15794266

WITHDRAWN

HENRY JAMES
AND
THE EVOLUTION
OF
CONSCIOUSNESS

HENRY JAMES
AND
THE EVOLUTION
OF
CONSCIOUSNESS

A Study of
The Ambassadors

by
Courtney Johnson, Jr.

Michigan State University Press
1987

The paper used in this publication meets the minimum require-
ments of American National Standard for Information Sciences—
Permanence of Paper for Printed Library Materials ANSI Z39.48-
1984.

Michigan State University Press
East Lansing, Michigan 48824

Editing: Pauline Sondag
Design & Production: Julie L. Loehr
Typeset in TEX by DigiGraphics, Inc., East Lansing, MI
Printing: Edwards Brothers, Ann Arbor, MI

Library of Congress Cataloging in Publication Data

Johnson, Courtney
    Henry James and the evolution of consciousness.

    Includes bibliographical references and index.
    1. James, Henry, 1843–1916. Ambassadors. 2. James, Henry,
1843–1916—Knowledge—Psychology. 3. Consciousness in
literature. I. Title.
PS2116.A53J64   1987)   813'.4   86-63236
ISBN 0-87013-245-8 (alk. paper)

Dedicated to
BMJ

CONTENTS

Acknowledgments

I am deeply grateful to the following professors who read carefully and made critical suggestions on this book: Lyall H. Powers and Sheridan Baker of the University of Michigan; Howard Anderson, Reed Baird and Lev Raphael of Michigan State University; and Rhoda Orme-Johnson of Maharishi International University. I am especially grateful to Professor Anderson for encouraging me to start the book in the first place and continuing to encourage me all throughout its development. I am also grateful to Jeffrey Ritter, Assistant to the Director of the Ayur Vedic Clinic of Lancaster, Massachusetts, for his splendid contribution to the scientific theory of Strether's motivation in the Appendix, and to Daniel Mark Fogel of Louisiana State University for his meticulous reading of my second chapter.

I am also most grateful to John C. Hagelin and Ashley Deans of the M.I.U. Physics Department for instructing me in the unified field theory and editing my rendition of the same. To Jean Blair, retired Director of the M.S.U. Press, I owe much gratitude for encouraging the M.S.U. Foundation to select this as the one work to be published by an M.S.U. faculty member for the year and for working with me patiently for months; also my thanks to Richard Chapin, the current Director, for his cooperation and help throughout the completion of the book, and the Assistant to the Director, Julie Loehr.

I am most grateful to Jo Grandstaff who typed and retyped the manuscript and made all manner of helpful suggestions; to Pauline Sondag for her sensitive and careful editing; to Karyn Dombrowski for organizing a major part of the indexing; and finally to my wife Beatrice (Dollie) Johnson for her undying support and understanding during the composition of the book, sustained despite the fact that even now she doubts it will ever be finished.

PREFACE

> . . . the moral event that takes place in the breast of the ambassador, his change of mind...can only be reached through Strether's consciousness . . . .
>
> —Percy Lubbock, *The Craft of Fiction*

Serious readers of Henry James, the master psychological novelist, have long recognized the importance of *consciousness* in his works and especially in *The Ambassadors*—"quite the best, all round," he thought, of his productions. The attention of critics has been focused on consciousness, as on its complementary narrative technique of "point of view," since W. Morton Fullerton wrote (with the adroit assistance of Edith Wharton) his important review of the New York Edition of James's novels and tales in 1910. There Fullerton pondered James's contribution to the development of the art of fiction:

> The most fruitful of these innovations was the principle that the action of each narrative should be recorded in the consciousness of one or more of the actors rather than in the vague impersonal register of an *ex machina* story-teller. Mr. James had learned, in other words, that the only way of acquiring the objectivity necessary to artistic representation was to assume successively, and at the exact "psychological moment," the states of mind of the actors *through whom his story became a story.*

A decade later the young Percy Lubbock produced his seminal study of the Jamesian tradition, *The Craft of Fiction*. In his extended

commentary on *The Ambassadors* Lubbock makes the observation
that Lambert Strether,

> with a mind working so diligently upon every grain of his
> experience, is a most luminous painter of the world in which
> he moves . . . standing above the story and taking a broad view
> of many things, . . . transcending the limits of the immediate
> scene . . . . The man's mind has become visible, phenomenal,
> dramatic; but in acting its part it still lends us eyes, is still an
> opportunity of extended vision. (149)

In more recent years some memorable moments in criticism of
The Ambassadors and of the role of consciousness in James's work
have been provided by such critics as Tony Tanner and Joseph A.
Ward, and the brilliant *tour de force* of Ian Watt's study of the
opening paragraph of *The Ambassadors.* So in view of the early
interest in the topic and the sustained and more recently quite rich
treatment of it, one might well ask what justification can be offered
for yet another study of consciousness in James's premier fiction.

Good as much of the criticism of James's psychological fiction
has been, even the best analyses of *The Ambassadors* seem to stop just
short of a fully satisfactory exegesis: they seem to lead us confidently
and persuasively to a certain point, but only so far—beyond that
we are left with a vexing confusion of discord and disagreement.
Many interesting studies devoted principally to narrative technique,
particularly to the function of Strether's point of view, are satisfying
as far as they go. Engaging claims have been bravely made for *The
Ambassadors* in terms of James's own praise of Flaubert's *Madame
Bovary:* "The form is in *itself* as interesting, as active, as much
of the essence of the subject as the idea, and yet so close is its
fit and so inseparable its life that we catch it at no moment on
any errand of its own. . . . Emma interests us by the nature of her
consciousness and the play of her mind . . . " (*Notes on Novelists*
475–77). Even the best of these endeavors founder, alas, when they
have finally to declare what "the idea" of *The Ambassadors* really
is, what the wonderfully appropriate form of this novel contrives
at last to express—what, in fact, this anything but loose and baggy
creature actually does *mean.*

In spite of all, then, what we still await is a critical demonstration that can persuasively move our understanding and appreciation
of *The Ambassadors* the necessary step further. We await the kind of
"breakthrough" that seems quite regularly to punctuate the progress
of scientific research and to be comparatively rare in literary study.

I do not refer to such events as the recent "discovery" of an important cache of letters by Edith Wharton that cast fresh light on such matters as her affair with Morton Fullerton—extremely useful as that discovery will prove to be. I have in mind something in the order of Leon Edel's stunning demonstration of some years ago to the Modern Language Association of "The Architecture of the New York Edition." That essay is a brilliant performance that relies on keen critical perception and solid breadth of literary scholarship.

I believe that Courtney Johnson's study of Henry James and the evolution of consciousness is just such a literary breakthrough and affords another stunning enlargement of our vision and sharpening of our appreciation of James's achievement. His study is likewise based on clarity of critical perception and solid scholarship, literary and otherwise—for it benefits from the additional support of impressive (and somewhat surprising) extra-literary authority.

Mr. Johnson's point of departure is a consideration of Henry James's relationship to the psychology and pragmatism of his brother William James. In so doing he follows to some extent the very helpful introduction to that matter provided by Richard A. Hocks in his *Henry James and Pragmatistic Thought*. Johnson then consults James's nonfiction prose, and in particular the arresting essay of 1910 entitled "Is There a Life After Death?"—which is replete with important comment on consciousness. The principal focus of the essay is given emphasis in such passages as this:

> Whatever we may begin with we almost inevitably go on, under the discipline of life, to more or less resigned acceptance of the grim fact that "science" takes no account of the soul, the principle we worry about, and that, as however nobly thinking and feeling creatures, we are abjectly and inveterately shut up in our material organs. (205)

As he develops his argument, James explains the importance for him of his consciousness—the soul, of which "science" takes no account—and drives to the ringing affirmation of his conclusion, "I reach beyond the laboratory brain" (232).

The ensuing discussion of consciousness is impressively aided by Johnson's turning to the tradition of serious meditation and invoking testimony of meditators such as the *rishis* or seers of the ancient *Bhagavad-Gita* of India as well as the experienced and trained meditators of the present day. Their experiences clearly parallel Lambert Strether's as recorded in *The Ambassadors*. He is thus able to go beyond the familiar concerns of the critics of "psychological fiction"—the role of ordinary consciousness—to a consideration of pure or transcendental consciousness. (In this pursuit he sheds new light on the question of James's debt to Swedenborg—via the religious philosophy of Henry James, Sr. or otherwise—and, evidently, to William Blake as well.) He is thus appealing to the support of what has seemed to be the *least* scientific pole of the spectrum of human study. And that, as might be expected from the nature of James's fiction and the explicit thrust of his essay on life after death, is quite as it should be.

The exciting new dimension in this discussion of consciousness results from Johnson's invoking supplementary testimony from what would appear to be the opposite pole of the spectrum of human study, that of science itself. First, he offers this testimony in the light of scientific studies on meditators, demonstrating that transcendental consciousness is a verifiable experience. Later he affirms an equivalence of the field of pure or transcendental consciousness achieved by meditators and the unified field of physics, which experts in that field say is the basis of all nature. In discovering to us that both pursuits are in fact scientific processes, he affords a resolution of their apparent opposition. In very abbreviated form, the reason Johnson gives for the equation of the unified field and transcendental consciousness is as follows:

> On a theoretical level, the intellect at one time seemed to be based very fundamentally on time, space and causation. But with the quantum theory of the unified field, there is no ability to distinguish past and future. Time diminishes or virtually disappears; and space manifests itself in such a way that to define distance in a classical sense seems impossible. Thus there is absolutely no place for the intellect to put its foot. It seems it is not the domain of the intellect to function outside of space and time, but rather of some structure of knowledge itself causally prior to space and time. In terms of the mind, that structure of knowledge is to be found in transcendence, which takes the mind beyond space and time. In order to live the total potential of natural law, one must take the attention to . . . pure or nonvibrating consciousness, where all the laws of nature are fully enlivened. (See Appendix, 145)

Einstein and the authors of the *Bhagavad-Gita* of India now join hands as they are shown to be of one mind, concerned with one being.

In applying the result of this fusion of the nonscientific and the scientific to his analysis of *The Ambassadors*, Johnson is able to achieve what I have called his "breakthrough"; on the basis of this perception—that the field of pure consciousness as experienced in Strether's mind is the unified field of physics—he is able to provide an explication of *The Ambassadors* (and, more briefly, of *The Portrait of a Lady*) that more fully satisfies our understanding of its "idea" and more vividly awakens our appreciation of James's masterfully controlling and expressive form.

The development of Johnson's analysis is a complex affair. It could hardly be otherwise: at issue here is a highly complex matter. The exegesis is necessarily reiterative in style. The same ground seems to be covered and recovered; quotations recur. But this is *intentional*. The repetition is *incremental*; and the development of the argument is *cumulative*. The exegesis demands patience and alert attention, but the patient and attentive reader will find the reward commensurate with the demand.

Johnson addresses directly the old problems raised by the conclusion of *The Ambassadors*: "are Strether and James *really* (a Bostonian 'really') condoning adultery?" and "what has made Strether act in such a strange way toward Chad and Marie de Vionnet and in such a 'disappointing' way toward Maria Gostrey?" and "what can Strether look forward to upon his return to Woollett?" I think that the reader will find that Johnson's handling of these questions is persuasive and satisfying and that it takes us a substantial step beyond the best answers proffered to date. His exposition is carefully argued and generously illustrated. His conciliatory approach to the canon of commentary embraces thorough consideration of other Jamesian scholars and critics. There is little of the polemical in his proceedings: his practice is generous and genial, rather, in that it tends to involve and utilize the comments of others to the end of "improving" their perceptions and clarifying their conclusions as he allows them their contributive place in his own commanding vision of the work in question and his conception of its significance.

In addition to all of that, there is something quite engaging in the atmosphere of excitement and delight that attends much of Johnson's explication; it is the thrill of convinced discovery and the joyful compulsion to share it with the universe. That quality of his style gives us the sense, surely, of what it must be like to experience the spirit of clarified vision that Lambert Strether is evidently imbued with—the spirit that raises (if only occasionally) ordinary mortals into the realm of the inspired artist. On this phenomenon James observes in "Is There a Life After Death?":

> I deal with being, . . . and in so doing I find myself—I can't express it otherwise—in communication with *sources*; sources to which I owe the apprehension of far more and far other combinations than observation and experience, in their ordinary sense, have given me the pattern of.
>
>   . . . The very provocation offered to the artist by the universe, the provocation to him to *be* . . . an artist, and thereby supremely serve it; what do I take that for but the intense desire of being to get itself personally shared, to show itself for personally sharable, and thus foster the sublimest faith? (224–25)

That, by the way, is a late echo of the condition of his early artist-hero Benvolio (in the story of that name, published in 1875): "if, being near him, you had been able to listen intently enough, he would, like the great people of his craft, have seemed to emit something of that vague magical murmur—the voice of the infinite . . . " (357).

Faith in the sanctity of that murmur, conveyed to him in actual life through the lips of his guardian angel, "mon bon," moved James to defend the desires of his "soul," his consciousness, against the commands of "science" and to utter that convinced affirmation— "I reach beyond the laboratory-brain." Courtney Johnson seems to have been moved by a similar murmur and led to reach even beyond the agon of "soul" and "science" to reconcile consciousness and the laboratory-brain. And his critical elucidation of the work of Henry James persuades us that the Master too must have glimpsed such a reconciliation himself without, however, being totally aware, in the intellectual sense, of what he had apprehended.

Lyall H. Powers
The University of Michigan

INTRODUCTION

If one examines the criticism of *The Ambassadors* over the past 30 or so years, one finds a wide discrepancy in the way it has been interpreted; so wide, in fact, that one wonders what to make of it all. One writer says Strether's refusal to marry Maria Gostrey is "precisely dreadful" and, in fact, everything concerning Strether can be summed up with one word: "folly" (Holland 281). Yet another writer says Strether's new vision is a "composed universe." He achieves "visionary" moments, and his view of Europe is one of "sublimity" and "magnificence" (Ward 354). Hardly a meeting of minds here.[1]

Perhaps the reason for such wide discrepancies in interpretation is that something has been omitted, something that becomes increasingly apparent as one singles it out and begins to study it throughout the novel. Henry James was interested in consciousness throughout his career, and he shaped his work in terms of his discoveries about consciousness and his knowledge of how it functions. In

---

[1] The discrepancies go on: Robert McLean says Strether recognizes, in his last meeting with Marie de Vionnet, that she is "a pathetically aging woman, the victim of a hopeless and vulgar passion"; while F. O. Mathiessen says "James has succeeded in making [her] so attractive that . . . there can be no question of Strether's caring for any other woman . . . and she is a goddess" (39).

F. C. Crews says Strethers's success is "entirely on an intellectual level" (36); while Robert E. Long in direct opposition says Strether overcomes his ingrained Puritanism by his growing awareness to sense experience.

the last three novels he wrote, he created characters—at least two, Lambert Strether and Maggie Verver, and possibly a third, Merton Densher—who most critics would agree undergo a transformation in the course of their lives and end up as unusually excellent examples of human nature, or of "fine consciousness."

Working with *The Ambassadors*, the book that James thought his best, and the one that offers the clearest example of this transformation to "fine" or "extra-ordinary" consciousness, I have made a study of the transformation in character of its hero, Lambert Strether. In approaching the study I discovered that the "extra-ordinary" consciousness appearing in James's fiction is also consciously and explicitly described in one of his essays and also in a number of his brother William's essays. During their lives, though as novelist and psychologist they employed different forms of communication, both writers formulated the notion (a notion based on their *experience* of consciousness) that there are two distinct levels or states functioning in the mind. Both writers refer to the first level as "ordinary" consciousness, but they use various terms to refer to the second. Sometimes William calls it simply "higher" consciousness, sometimes "pure experience." Henry recollects experiencing an area in the mind containing "sources." Throughout the text, I associate all these terms with transcendent states of the mind. Also, the term "extra-ordinary" is not unfaithful to the terminology of either Henry or William as a reference to the second level of consciousness. For the present, except in quotations, I will use these terms to indicate the second level wherever possible.

It is very likely that Henry James did experience that state his brother explicitly refers to as "higher consciousness." In Henry's case, the essay I am referring to came late in his career. In that essay, he discusses extra-ordinary consciousness with reference to his own personal life. Unfortunately, he does not tell us when the earliest experience or any other such experience occurred except in most general terms. He appears to have constructed certain characters in his novels on the basis of such experiences in his own life. It is this probable use of extra-ordinary consciousness in his fiction, and the epistemological implications it involves, that persuaded me to make this study.

The "higher consciousness" that William James refers to repeatedly (and Henry occasionally) is, according to the experts, a particular type of awareness that everyone has a potential for, but it is only rarely manifested or maintained in everyday life. After William

James's speculations early in this century, scientific investigation of the subject was minimal until some twenty to twenty-five years ago. Since that time, experiments on higher (extra-ordinary) consciousness have increased and been conducted on a world-wide basis. In laboratory tests, scientists noted distinct physiological changes in persons during periods of apparent extra-ordinary consciousness. These tests marked those persons capable of achieving this unusual level. When interviewed, the subjects related diverse experiences. At the same time, generally consistent among them was an overpowering sense of clear awareness of the inner self. Associated with this was a feeling of omniscience, ease, and effortlessness, particularly in regard to obtaining one's goals. The long-term experiments indicate that such experiences can be the beginning of a permanently expanded state of awareness, or one stage in the development toward such permanence. Additional experiments confirm that this sustained realization gives a new, clearer meaning to the person's actions and a greater appreciation of life. Is there really evidence of such transformations occurring in James's later fiction?

Consider *The Ambassadors*. The hero in this novel at least undergoes a change that, in the course of his journey, makes him markedly different from what he had previously been. In the beginning he is overly dependent, lacks confidence in himself, is suspicious, and feels he has "missed" his life (he is 55). In the end he has matured. He has a far greater capacity to feel and to live. He is also fully confident, independent in his decisions, and, as he says himself, happy.

But in interpreting this change a few critics, among them J.A. Ward, while accepting the attributes of the change mentioned here would also see another capacity revealing itself. In the new capacity, which results from transcendence, the mind "goes beyond" its original, ordinary, limited state of awareness and achieves a second, separate level, not clearly evidenced before in the range of that person's experience. Though he does not use the term, Ward's description comes close to this definition: "Many complex effects result from the exposure of the protagonist [Strether] to such a setting [as he experiences in Paris], but, in the main, they tend to give him a vision of life that so fundamentally upsets his sense of the world and his own relation to it that he is converted into someone not just more refined or more aware, but different" (352). Ward cites William James's description of such a change as "the sense of 'an absolutely new nature breathed into us'" (353). Again,

R.W. Stallman sees Strether as realizing a new sense of time—a timeless level or condition of knowledge—in other words, a change resulting in a condition that is for all practical purposes opposite to the original one.

The point of all this is that if Strether's growth culminates in "extra-ordinary" consciousness—and if it is an identifiable state that differs from ordinary consciousness—then interpretation of the novel will have to take that condition into account. Such an accounting will be particularly necessary for understanding Strether at the end of the novel. Careful consideration of it should also hold the promise of clearing up the discrepancies in interpretation mentioned earlier.

My general aim in this book is to construct a model of evolving consciousness as it moves toward transcendent consciousness in The Ambassadors. After the comparison of the ideas of Henry and William in Chapter I, Chapter II analyzes the distinction between the two levels of consciousness—the ordinary and the extra-ordinary—in the hero, Lambert Strether. That second level begins to appear in him when he arrives in Europe, and it synchronizes with the first level with increasing intensity and clarity during the course of his visit. Consequently, the chapter goes on to indicate how the function of these levels and their interrelation underlie the structure of the novel as a whole. Parallel to this, the light imagery, primarily as it appears in Gloriani's garden, is most revealing as it opposes the ordinary light of Strether's day (his ordinary consciousness) that "marked his old geography" to the "personal lustre almost violent that shone in constellation" about Gloriani. The two kinds of light foreshadow the two kinds of consciousness that Strether will realize: the initial dim, benighted one and the subsequent brilliant, enlightened one.

The third chapter analyzes the "mechanics of transcendence" as a basis for the interrelationship of the two levels that appear in Strether's development. What does it mean to transcend? What literally happens? This chapter forms a groundwork for the development of the remaining chapters and the development of the de facto synthesis of the levels of consciousness in the hero. The concluding chapters afford an explanation of those puzzling choices he makes at the end.

THE INTELLECTUAL POSITION
OF THE BROTHERS

Henry James's pervading interest throughout his career as an artist was centered on the consciousness of his characters. He sometimes used the term "consciousness" interchangeably with "awareness." The study of consciousness in art form—which James's career could appropriately be called—began with the appearance, early in his novels and stories, of different types of consciousness as well as different "degrees" of consciousness. He frequently talked of "vessels" that contained different "amounts" of awareness (La Brie 520). James began to formulate a system in which a character of fine sensitivity (or potentially fine sensitivity) was made the center of consciousness of all the activity occurring in the story. The intention was that through him the novel might be unified and upon him everything might be made to depend. The "center of consciousness" characters, from one type of story to another, began to exhibit, not necessarily in perfect consistency, certain positive characteristics—a striking capacity to appreciate the surface of life and all the depths of it, a compassion accompanying this, and an objectivity. Finally, in the Major Phase, there appeared in Lambert Strether, Maggie Verver, and even Merton Densher a change of consciousness so extreme as to astonish other characters, as well as readers. Critics have described the change as a moral and aesthetic transformation, a transformation of vision, and if not a religious conversion then at least something akin to it. It seems possible that these transformations in the late characters are part of a natural evolution of consciousness—in the fictional consciousness of the character and the consciousness of James himself—that he saw as he moved into that stage.[1] In doing so, he realized certain types who had extraordinary appreciation and awareness in contrast with characters in earlier stories and novels who were, to James the artist, a mere preparation for the final brilliant portraits he gave us.

James puts this notion in his own words in the Preface to *The Princess Casamassima* that he wrote for the New York Edition (1908):

> I have . . . a weakness of sympathy [with George Eliot] to show the adventures [of characters] and their history—the author's subject-matter, all—as determined by their feelings and the nature of their minds . . . I should even like to give myself the pleasure of retracing from one of my own productions to another the play of a like instinctive disposition, of catching in the fact, at one point after another, from "Roderick Hudson" to "The Golden Bowl," that provision for interest which consists in placing advantageously, placing right in the middle of the light, the most polished of possible mirrors of the subject. Rowland Mallett, in "Roderick Hudson," is exactly such a mirror . . . Newman in *The American* . . . Isabel Archer in *The Portrait of a Lady* . . . Merton Densher in *The Wings of the Dove* . . . Lambert Strether in *The Ambassadors* (*he* a mirror verily of miraculous silver and quite pre-eminent, I think for the connection) . . . . These persons are . . . intense *perceivers*, all, of their respective predicaments, and I should go on from them to fifty other examples. [He gives about seven besides the above.] (*Art of the Novel* 62–63)

The Henry James essay, "Is There a Life After Death?" referred to in my Introduction, first appeared in *Harper's Bazaar*, January-February 1910, and afterward in a symposium on immortality in the same year.[2]

It is an account of what James considered important aspects of consciousness, including how it functions and how, over a period

---

[1] James often portrayed consciousness as being a state of motion. It was the movement in consciousness which made possible the drama of consciousness in the lives of his characters: "She (a projected character in a story whose name he has not yet fully determined, but he calls her 'Betty'!) has, in a word, a wholly changed consciousness, and the change is what I chronicle" (*Notebooks* 341).

[2] So far as I know R. A. Hocks (see this chapter, p. 13) was the first critic to recognize the remarkable character of many of James's statements in this essay.

of years, his position on the subject changed. It is also the most complete and explicit statement he ever made on the subject as it concerns the "extra-ordinary" level of consciousness. Because of this, and because of the precision James exercises in phrasing these concepts, I examine the essay here in some detail.

James begins by explaining how, in his early years, his life was so full that the question of an afterlife did not appeal to him, or, in his own words, "the aggression of this life was ready to fill the bill" (217).[3] That aggression dissolved questions which death might raise. However, after much time, he says, he began to get a picture of what it is to die, and particularly what it is [or must be] to *have died*. He then remarks, looking back over his life, on how our conception of reality changes. He gives an example of how this happened in his own case. He speaks of the world of appearances, in the Platonic sense, the world behind which lies substantial reality (217). Over a long period, these appearances kept proclaiming to him that, because of their finite nature and the resulting fragmentation of everything, the world could do perfectly well without such a fragmentary particle as himself or, for that matter, anyone he knew!

However, all the time he had been "taking the measure of [his] consciousness" on the basis of its being finite, he had also "learned to live in it more and more" (219–20). "I had doubtless taken thus to increased living in it by reaction against so grossly finite a world— for it (again, my consciousness) at least *contained* the world, and could handle and criticize it, could play with it and deride it; it had *that superiority*: which meant, all the while, such successful living that the abode itself grew more and more interesting to me, and with this beautiful sign of its character that the more one asked of it the more and the more it appeared to give" (220).

The phrase "contained the world," coupled with the phrase "learned to live in it," represents a change in understanding so large it is comparable to Copernicus's first viewing the sun as the center of the solar system. If consciousness is all we have to apprehend the world with, if consciousness contains the world, then to all intents and purposes it is the world, because what we do or know depends upon the condition of our consciousness. And if one can "criticize

---

[3] This aggression in turn is caused by what he calls "resented bereavement." He does not explain the term, but does it not mean, since bereavement so often involves resentment—anger—that we form a notion of death as the enemy, or as "something bad"? Again, at times it reflects the anger some people feel at the person who died, and that results in a similar attitude.

it," "play with it," and even "deride it," as Henry James says, then in a very real sense the control of one's comprehension, viewpoint, and knowledge of the world originates somewhere within one's own consciousness. Also, if consciousness grows, and the more we ask of it the more it gives, as he says, it is "more than" finite. It is infinite.

In this essay, Henry James depicts the mind as capable of extending its awareness beyond the limits of ordinary consciousness. He discusses the "extra-ordinary" consciousness in two ways: in connection with the present life and in connection with the afterlife. (I will limit myself mostly to the first, as it is the present life of Strether that I am ultimately concerned with.) He points out that the new ("extra-ordinary") condition is not something one accomplishes in one moment:

> It is not that I have found in growing older any one marked or momentous line in the life of the mind or in the play of the freedom of the imagination to be stepped over; but that a process takes place which I can only describe as the accumulation of the very treasure of consciousness itself. (221)

Shortly after this James refers to the place where he finds his "treasure" as a place of "sources" (224). These sources are, he says, "the fountain of creativity" (228); to these sources, he continues, "I owe the apprehension of more and far other combinations than observation and experience, in the ordinary sense, have given me the pattern of" (224).

In these statements, Henry James is making a remarkable assertion. He begins by saying a number of things about his own consciousness. Earlier he has said that it contains two functions (the ones I call ordinary and extra-ordinary); now he adds that one of the functions is based on experience, ordinary experience, and the other based upon something other than that. In the second, he says he apprehends far more than in the first. As the very "treasure of consciousness itself," the second is, if not the *most* valuable part, at least one *extremely* valuable part, of consciousness as a whole.

No one would question that, as he has portrayed them so far, these states are different from each other. But what is the critical nature of the difference? Is there anything about this new element so "wholly other" as to alter the nature of the first when and if the two come together? James answers this question in the following manner:

> I appreciate this 'beautiful and enjoyable' independence of
> thought [afforded by my "sources"] and more especially this assault
> of the boundlessly multiplied personal relation (my own), which
> carries me beyond even any 'profoundest' observation of this world
> whatever, and any mortal adventure, and refers me to realizations
> I am condemned as yet but to dream of. (223)

He ends here with a phrase quite similar to the one used in the
Project[4] and again in the Preface to The Ambassadors, where he said
in both cases that this "extra-ordinary" realm is beyond anything
the Strether of the "Woollett" philosophy ever dreamed of. The distinction has been made. The line is drawn. The "sources" are of the
"immortal" world. Comprehending them makes him realize things
he had never dreamed of. This whole idea sounds (and is) paradoxical, because he would appear to be having glimpses "beyond" what
he is supposed to, beyond sense experience, yet somehow these realizations have been initiated in the framework of the ordinary, or
in the framework of sense experience, only to progress to somewhere outside sense experience. He supports his own ambivalent
contention most strongly in the same essay when he describes the
senses collectively as a "frame" from which we learn "to plant, spiritually, our feet." And—if it is not already obvious—he admits his
conception "comes back to the theory . . . of orthodox theology"
(230). By personal experience—by an experimental approach that
can only be called pragmatic, James thus came to a view of epistemology that is well within the range of Christian dogma. He arrived
there, however, in his own private way, not through abstract doctrine, not through an inculcation of Judaeo-Christian theology. His
making this comparison is useful in that our general familiarity with
that system helps us get his into perspective.

   The essence of his argument is that there is an area of consciousness beyond the ordinary, beyond sense experience, which
(paradoxically) the mind can apprehend in spite of the fact that
"all our knowledge," as Kant said, "is grounded in experience." I do
not propose to resolve the corresponding paradox in James's essay
or his fiction, except to say it is evident, if one chooses to study
the text closely, that every moment of Lambert Strether's time and
every instance of his experience in Paris is imbued with paradox.
It is through the way his mind learns to treat such paradoxes, as a

---

[4] The term refers to Henry James's "Project of Novel" done and submitted to
Harper & Bros. in 1900.

number of critics have recently indicated, that Strether is ultimately able to be so thoroughly in possession of himself.[5] From that point in his essay, James reflects on a point in his life when his outlook changed from his feeling alone and apart from everything to his feeling very much a part of everything. The change is reflected in his philosophical views: he is on the verge of affirming an awareness that is both ever-increasing and unifying—ever-increasing because consisting of multiple relations that continually grow and unifying because steadily more coherent and all-inclusive. This condition might for the present be called "universal awareness." Notice how he addresses both the above points in the following quotations:

> I won't say the world, as we commonly refer to it, grows more attaching, but will say that the *universe increasingly does*, and this makes us present at the enormous multiplication of our possible relations with it . . . . (221)

Instead of living in a universe where all is fragmented, where, to achieve identity, one affixes himself to random fragments of it, he now finds the universe an enormous, connected whole; as we multiply our relations with it, we increasingly identify with it in its entirety. The scope or range of consciousness increases like an expanding sphere. At a certain point of growth one discovers, along with the *possibilities* of growth, a stabilizing and unifying influence on the *nature* of growth.

An oft-quoted image James used in "The Art of Fiction" describes the operation of consciousness in similar terms:

> Experience is never limited, and it is never complete; it is an immense sensibility, a kind of huge spider web of the finest silken threads suspended in the chamber of consciousness and catching every airborne particle in its tissue. It is the very atmosphere of the mind; and when the mind is imaginative—much more when it happens to be that of a man of genius—it takes to itself the faintest hints of life, it converts the very pulses of the air into revelations. (*Future of the Novel* 12)

This entire paragraph describes the function of ordinary consciousness until the last clause, in which what is probably the operation of "extra-ordinary" consciousness transforms the mind and all "impulses" around it into something entirely new.

---

[5] Daniel Fogel gives a concise but detailed and informative history of the problems of opposites and the synthesizing of opposites in James (Intro.).

Thus far James has affirmed certain things about his mind, and, indirectly perhaps, affirmed its appearance in minds other than his own. The "extra-ordinary" (1) is a place of sources; (2) is a place of immense value in life; (3) is the fountain of creativity; (4) has a quality of infinity; (5) has the capacity to go beyond the limits of ordinary consciousness or ordinary experience; (6) differs and is separate from the ordinary (this relation is a paradox which needs yet to be and will be more fully explained); and (7) is also, at the same time, stabilizing and unifying in its effect on the mind in general.

The implications of the paradox of a mind, whether in real life or fiction, experiencing both sense experience and something beyond that, are that man is either capable of functioning in two states or conditions (or systems of perception) at the same time, or that the two states are not *really* different, they just seem to be. This whole book rests on the position that *Henry James's* conception, as shown in his essay and in *The Ambassadors* itself, is that the two states are different from each other and separate as well (though they can function simultaneously and have a certain amount of correspondence).

Extra-ordinary consciousness is separate from ordinary consciousness in the same way that immortality is separate (and different) from mortality. This gives rise to a further equation, which is, how is the one (extra-ordinary) related to the other?[6]—and still another quite naturally follows, which is, how can two parts of such an obvious contradiction be reconciled? As a rule, these questions, in interpreting fiction, are not satisfactorily answered by an abstract argument. Especially in James and particularly in *The Ambassadors* they should be treated in terms that apply directly to the mind of the character, and I fully intend to approach them in this way. But a statement about the questions from James's personal experience would certainly add conviction to the literary analysis. James does give a glimpse of the nature of this relationship when he says earlier in "Is There a Life After Death?" that consciousness "*contained* the world" (220). With this in mind, once we have an idea of his "sources" or the "extra-ordinary" faculties that he later mentions, we can see how extra-ordinary consciousness can be imagined as an outer ring (or again, an upper atmosphere) surrounding and

---

[6] Ross La Brie says that to James there is something (the faculty of consciousness) "that proceeds from the writer and transcends the writer at the same time" (518). Both meanings are relevant to James's idea of consciousness.

containing ordinary consciousness, just as the physical atmosphere "contains" the earth, or just as the substance of immortality, in the-ological terms, might contain, or might be a vast support system wrapped around a central "sphere" designated by the term "mortal-ity." In this way, immortality could be said to contain mortality, or extra-ordinary consciousness to contain ordinary or eternity contain temporality. The "atmosphere" holds up the sphere, and even pen-etrates it whenever possible, to cause an expansion of awareness, as William's remarks which follow demonstrate.

Henry James has said so far that, provided one is able to capture the more elusive or "extra-ordinary" element in his mind and sustain it, the mind gains a stabilizing factor. To the degree that extra-ordinary consciousness penetrates or transforms or simply influences ordinary consciousness, and to the degree that such consciousness expands or enlarges one's awareness, it creates greater stability in the person or character. This happens because, with the advent of the new consciousness, one's consciousness as a whole now includes both aspects of reality, the ordinary and the extra-ordinary, or the finite and the infinite, or the here and now *plus* the beyond. If the various pairs should synthesize, the result would be a balanced mind whose awareness continually grows more inclusive (of reality— extra-ordinary and otherwise), more stable, and more "universal."

Let me illustrate this last point further. To return to the "multiplication of possible relations," it is possible to say James's description involves a view of the mind in which thought, feelings, anything in consciousness, begins at a hypothetical core. As growth continues, relationships join and expand and join and expand from the core in an ever-widening circle, always enabling the mind to form newer relations until one finds himself experiencing a second, less obvious circle of consciousness outside the perimeter of the original one. James says this ever-widening growth leads to an "unlimited vision of being," which is another way of saying that, whether through intuition or divine revelation or other as yet unknown faculties, one is becoming aware of everything in existence, even the third universe over from this one (not as to fact but as to form). In the same essay he says (this time addressing the artist in himself and others):

> It is in a word the artistic consciousness and privilege in itself that thus shines as from immersion in the fountain of being. Into that fountain, to depths immeasurable, our spirit dips—to the effect of feeling itself, *qua* imagination and aspiration, all scented

with universal sources. (228)

Before applying the information gained from his essay to Henry James's work, let us first take into account one further piece of evidence, provided by his brother William, that indicates Henry James did indeed experience the growth of this "extra-ordinary" consciousness, that he pictured it as "outside" ordinary consciousness, *and* that the two states nonetheless had an interrelationship that William pictures for us in a most clarifying way.

The terminology of Henry James's 1910 essay—"sources," "treasures," etc.—may seem a trifle vague; but a review of key passages in William's publications between 1896 and 1910 casts a ray of clarification on Henry's terms. To do so is really quite legitimate, as R.A. Hocks' study of the ideas of the two brothers has clearly established.[7] The fundamental ideas of Henry and William James were remarkably similar during almost all of their respective lives. In his searching comparison of the attitude of both men over fifty or more years, Hocks points out that Henry's ideas, particularly as they pertain to epistemological constructs, were "dramatized" for us or came by implied statement, whereas William's, appearing in the more explicit language of philosophy and psychology, were discursive. Yet the two men have "a fundamental epistemological identification" (31). Hocks studies the two, not in terms of "influences," not in terms of "the history of ideas," but in terms of the history of consciousness (8). The result is a kind of parallel evolution that enhances our understanding of one brother in terms of the other.

For instance, on the subject of "extra-ordinary" consciousness, William says in the famous conclusion to *The Varieties of Religious Experience*:

> . . . Apart from all religious considerations there is actually and literally more life in our total soul than we are at any time aware of. The exploration of the transmarginal field has hardly yet been seriously undertaken, but what Mr. [F.W.H.] Myers said in 1892 in his essay on "Subliminal Consciousness," is as true as when it was first written:
>
> Each of us [says Myers], is in reality an abiding psychical entity far more extensive than he knows—an individuality which can never express itself completely through any corporeal manifestation. The self manifests itself through the organism; but there is always some part of the self unmanifested, and always, as it

---

[7] I am greatly indebted to Mr. Hocks for his initial selections of many of these passages in the works of William James (212–17).

seems, some power of organic expression in abeyance or reserve. (501–02)

In the essay, "What Psychical Research Has Accomplished," William says, "The ordinary consciousness Mr. Myers likens to the visible part of the solar spectrum; the total consciousness is like that spectrum prolonged by the inclusion of the ultrared and ultraviolet rays. In the psychic spectrum the 'ultra' parts may embrace a far wider range, both of physiological and of psychical activity, than is open to our ordinary consciousness and memory."

He says about this concept that there is a certain correspondence of the two levels, the ordinary and the ultra-violet-and-red (or "extra-ordinary"). "The result [of this proposal about the self] is to make me feel that we all have potentially a subliminal self, which may make at any time irruption into our ordinary lives" (*Will to Believe* 316–21).

The "ultra" area outside the solar spectrum, the "subliminal self," would seem to correspond precisely to the area described by Henry James when he speaks of the "freed imagination" accumulating the "very treasure of consciousness itself." Also both describe that outer area as if it were a "place outside," i.e., separate and different from ordinary consciousness, a "place" or "inspiration," or "universal" sources. It is (in Henry) the place where things have their origin, and where (in William) "the genuine matter of reality" is to be found.

"Suppose . . . that the whole universe of material things—the furniture of earth and choir of heaven—should turn out to be a mere surface-veil of phenomena, hiding and keeping back the world of genuine realities," says William in "Human Immortality," as he begins this totally revealing and detailed picture of the two worlds of consciousness. He quotes two lines of Shelley:

> "Life, like a dome of many-colored glass,
> Stains the white radiance of eternity."

Then he continued:

Suppose that the dome, opaque enough at all times to the full super-solar blaze, could at certain times and places grow less so, and let certain beams pierce through into this sublunary world. These beams would be so many finite rays, so to speak, of consciousness, and they would vary in quantity and quality as the opacity varied in degree. Only at particular times and places would it seem that, as a matter of fact, the veil of nature can grow thin and rupturable enough for such effects to occur. But in those places gleams, however finite and unsatisfying, of the absolute life of the universe, are from time to time vouchsafed. Glows of feeling, glimpses of insight, and streams of knowledge and perception float into our finite world.

Admit now that *our brains* are such thin and half-transparent places in the veil. What will happen? Why, as the white radiance comes through the dome, with all sorts of staining and distortion imprinted on it by the glass . . . even so the genuine matter of reality, the life of souls as it is in its fullness, will break through our several brains into this world in all sorts of restricted forms, and with all the imperfections and queernesses that characterize our finite individualities here below. (15–17)

Finally, he gives us a picture of the texture of that ultraviolet/red area in *Essays in Radical Empiricism*:

My thesis is that if we start with the supposition that there is only one primal stuff or material in the world, a stuff of which everything is composed, and if we call that stuff 'pure experience,' then knowing can easily be explained as a particular sort of relation toward one another into which portions of pure experience may enter. The relation itself is a part of pure experience; one of its 'terms' becomes the subject or bearer of the knowledge, the knower, the other becomes the object known. (4)

The world of pure experience is both different and separate from the ordinary world, but accessible to that world; in fact, portions of it may enter the ordinary world. In Henry's terms, to gain William's world of pure experience requires the realization and acquisition of "sources." The world of "sources" eventually becomes the stabilizing factor of the elements of the mind; that world is unchanging and eternal; the other, ordinary world, is transient and temporary.

If the "sources" could be the stabilizing and unifying element in consciousness, as Henry James affirms about his experience, does the same or a similar morphology of consciousness appear in his fiction, especially in *The Ambassadors*? In his Preface to *The Ambassadors* (1–3), James suggests that the novel has two basic elements in its construction: unity and diversity. Though he also refers to them as "stability in flux," or "germ lurking in the mass," or "seed in the garden," all are variations on the theme of a stability [of consciousness] achieved through unity, a unity that is ultimately illustrated by the consciousness of Lambert Strether, whose mind increasingly carries combinations of unity in diversity. And James says "the major property [observed by me in composing this book] was that of employing but one center all within my hero's compass" (9). I interpret this in *The Ambassadors* as a center which acted as a focal point for all the plot lines. In other words, the book employs a principle of composition whose aim it is to center everything in the hero's mind, and to have the hero's mind, in turn, achieve unity, or "stability in the midst of flux," as a resolution of the drama, which indeed is a drama of consciousness.

A logical question arises: when we look at the novel closely and then consider the claim in the Preface that its purpose is "unity," does that mean that the various components, like building blocks, come together in a neat sphere or cube or octagon or does he mean that the thoughts—the meanings—all combine to form an organic whole whose sum is greater than its parts? The latter is true, because the meaning of *The Ambassadors* is *entirely* rooted in the concept of unity, or, to make the term compatible with the essay, rooted in "unified consciousness."

Let me reiterate the possibility that consciousness has two levels in *The Ambassadors*, ordinary and extra-ordinary. As I will show, ordinary consciousness in the novel is associated with the complexity, the activity, and the "noise" of everyday living, while extra-ordinary consciousness is associated with the simplicity, the inactivity, and the silence of the transcendent experience. Take a hypothetical situation: having transcended ordinary consciousness, the mind experiences the "silence" (and inactivity) or "pure" (and harmonious) consciousness. After a time the mind leaves that state and returns to its everyday, active condition, in which it remains until the next episode of transcendence. Then, after a sufficient number of experiences of moving into and out of transcendental consciousness, after enough "mini-revolutions," the conditions of that transcendent consciousness will persist and become dominant in the person or literary character during everyday life. (This is in capsule a development I shall describe in detail in Chapter III.)

In numerous scenes, beginning with his first arrival in Paris, Strether's consciousness undergoes "mini-revolutions" leading to a greater stabilizing and unifying of the scattered elements of his existence. Let us look for a moment at just one: Strether's first full realization of the significance of the change he experienced in Paris, where James evokes the image of the Babes in the Wood to signify a sense of absolute peace that is overwhelming his hero. At this point, the series of transcendences he has been experiencing, followed by a return to everyday thinking, as if the experiences were stepping stones, is affecting him in a complete way and perhaps permanently. The scene I have in mind is Strether's visit with Maria Gostrey just after the boat scene near the end of the novel (345; 12, III). What precedes this is the following: he has been mentioning a sense of happiness, whose specific quality is composure, and signifies "a finer harmony of things; nothing but what had turned out as yet according to his plan" (320; 11, III). He began "to remember further still in subsequent meditations, many things that, as it were, fitted together" (328). As a result of the boat scene in which he discovers the deception of his friends, one would expect his composure to be shaken, but it is not, because his new state of mind—the condition of "silence"—is now too deeply established in him. He is, in fact, becoming *more* composed. He goes on to say he and Maria were like "Babes in the Wood"; they "could trust the elements to let them continue at peace" (345; 12, III). Then he says: "he might for all the world have been going to die . . . the scene was filled for him with so deep a death-bed hush." Very little of this phrasing refers to actual physical death, but to the quieting of the hero's physical and mental condition, a composure that is extreme in contrast to any earlier state of his consciousness. At the moment, his return to face Woollett has, he says, been postponed; when it happens, "One would float to it doubtless . . . through these caverns of Kubla Khan . . . he was to see, at best, what Woollett would be with everything there changed for him" (345–46).

His mind now is in possession of two conditions: the old, ordinary one of Woollett and the new, extra-ordinary one of Paris. In mentioning his Kubla Khan-like condition, the author appropriates a poem whose whole thrust is creation, renaissance, and immortality, a large measure of which belongs to Strether now. He is declaring that he has one more stage in his realization, which will come to him at Woollett. It will be an integration of old and new, of "Woollett" and "Paris," when he finally confronts "Woollett" with the result of his transformation. Not obvious perhaps is the realization he has reached already, that everything is part of everything else; yet he is not cemented to the past or future—he is living in the now.

> He wishes not to do anything because he had missed some-
> thing else, because he was sore or sorry or impoverished, because
> he was maltreated or desperate; he wished to do everything be-

cause he was *lucid and quiet, just the same for himself on all essential points as he had ever been.* (346; 12, III; emphasis mine)

Strether in his own mind is close to a condition of stability wedded to unity, a stability and unity of mind apart from his actual return, as appears in this imaginary one, in which he will integrate further as his present condition confronts and interprets more experience in Woollett. The combination, emanating from the new, "extra-ordinary" aspect of his consciousness, will permeate and affect everything he does.

Henry James's terminology in *his* essay on immortality can now be seen as quite appropriate for describing Strether's situation: Strether has reached (by eruptions or incursions or whatever means) the "source area" often enough or over long enough intervals of time that whatever "stuff" or "material" that source area contains, it has now (in Book 12) usurped the dominating position in his ordinary consciousness.

The process occurs for Lambert Strether in a series of stages chiefly represented in scenes with the Countess de Vionnet. The first sign of any transcendence occurs in Gloriani's garden; afterwards he has a number of similar experiences, all leading up to the scene with Maria that I have been referring to here. When all these changes are over, presumably the person has changed. What will such a person be like? To conceive of the difference let us imagine that we could enter the mind of a character and, using a powerful light, saturate every particle, every neuron, of his mind with light beams. Afterwards, when the character turned his attention to anything, he would see it only as filtered through the light. Everything not only would look quite different from the way it had before, but it would *be* different for him.

The succeeding chapters give a fully developed picture of how it would be different. But perhaps the following partial idea will help explain the general result at which the light image is aimed. To the "ordinary" active consciousness of the hero, add the consciousness that is discovered through transcendence, i.e., the "extra-ordinary." Transcendental consciousness can be associated with stability; and now also with stability comes a strong sense of independence, calm, and freedom. When the transformation in the character is complete, the qualities of the second state are found functioning along with the qualities of the first in such a way that every response to, say, noise (or sound in general) is accompanied by an underlying condition of silence; every impulse to act in a character is accompanied by an underlying condition of rest and order—thus *stability* appears when the two sides are in proper ratio. Why this happens, what it means, and what it has to do with transcendence in a complete sense, I have yet to show. However, the above hints that the transcendent element combined with ordinary consciousness may act as a ballast that, if present in Strether, can help him cope with any situation in life. The combination strongly affects, for example, his reaction to what he has learned about Marie and Chad's affair at the most critical point in the novel when his consciousness suddenly manifests a far greater understanding than we would expect from a man of "Woollett" who had never been to "Paris."

Seven years after publishing *The Ambassadors*, James wrote a passage at the end of the immortality essay, "Is There a Life After Death?" that reveals a double consciousness similar to the one in the scene above. It describes a stability and unity that emanate from the "sources" of consciousness found both in the essay and the text of the novel. He wrote:

> [I find our personality] not unlike the sustaining frame on little wheels that often encases growing infants, so that, dangling and shaking about in it, they may feel their assurance of walking increase and teach their small toes to know the ground. I like to think that we here, as to soul, dangle from the infinite and shake about in the universe; that this world and this conformation and these senses are our helpful and ingenious frame, amply provided with wheels and replete with the lessons for us of how to plant, spiritually, our feet. (229–30)

THE "INEXORABLE TIDE OF LIGHT"

Three years after completing *The Ambassadors*, Henry James, in his Preface to the New York Edition, took a long look at the scope and principle of the novel he thought to be "quite the best" of his productions. Early in the Preface (1) he refers to the famous garden passage of Book 5, II and says it contains "few words," but these words are "planted or 'sunk,' stiffly or saliently, in the center of a current." They form a stable element in a more or less fluctuating medium, a kind of center around which everything else revolves.

The few words to which he is referring are words of advice Lambert Strether, the hero of *The Ambassadors*, gives to John Little Bilham. He has met Bilham, a young American living in Paris, while on his own mission there to bring home an errant young man who is the son of an old friend. The setting for Strether's famous words—a party in a beautiful garden, a great sculptor as host, a countess who makes a deep impression on Strether—all elicit a sudden emotional outburst:

> . . . don't forget that you're young—blessedly young; be glad of
> it . . . and live up to it. Live all you can; it's a mistake not to.
> It doesn't so much matter what you do in particular, so long as
> you have your life. If you haven't had that what *have* you had?
> This place and these impressions . . . have had their abundant
> message for me, have just dropped *that* into my mind. I see it
> now. I haven't done so before—and now I'm old; too old at any
> rate for what I see. Oh, I *do* see, at least; and more than you'd
> believe or I can express. (137; 5, II)

In the Preface, James enlarges on his principle. He refers to a composition, the total composition of the book, which he says springs from a simple source, the very words just mentioned: "Never can a composition of this sort have sprung straighter from a dropped grain of suggestion; and never can that grain, developed, outgrown, and smothered, have yet lurked more in the mass as an independent particle" (1). The grain, or the few words of the speech, he says, though it is the "source" of the composition, nevertheless at this point in the development of the story appears in such a spontaneous manner that it is seen as independent—not yet integrated into the "mass"—of forthcoming ingredients.

This little fragment of a description—in the very broadest sense the *principle* of what James calls "the story of one's story" (5)— suggests the basic idea around which the inner story of Strether's experiences in Paris revolves. That principle is simple: unity in diversity. The author states that one fundamental element, a "stable" one, is related to every other part of the story, and every other part of the story to it.

"The remarks," he says (those remarks that contain the dropped grain), "contain the essence of 'The Ambassadors' [and now he is talking about Strether himself]; his fingers close, before he has done, round the stem of the full-blown flower, which, after that fashion, he continues officiously to present to us" (1). The whole novel, he suggests, grows out of one seed and grows in its conception like a flower. The story is first of all in the little seed, but during that moment with little Bilham, as "his fingers close," Strether gets an inkling of the whole and final creation, the magnificent blossoming, not just of a story about his present self but of something new about to develop in his life. And since flower emerges from seed, the two are now, in his description, integrated, or connected. Then James says: "Nothing can exceed the closeness with which the whole fits again into its germ" (2). The seed is not simply the flower's integral source, but, no matter how richly or wildly the flower may bloom, it can always *fit back* into the seed.

What does he mean?

Let us imagine several fine, wiry lines like fibers growing out of a core. In the course of the story, the seed or core will give out countless fibers like these, and as James's narrator tells the story, these fibers will become images and thoughts and activities that form the parts. Yet all the fibers growing from the center will ultimately be containable in the center itself. True, they will appear to have much more variety and flexibility than the center; yet they originated there, and their origin is whole and stable, not diverse and scattered like the branching fibers. They should fit back into the core in the sense that the core holds the potentiality of their completion and fulfillment, as in Aristotle's entelechy.

James rounds out this point by saying he adopted "a small compositional law . . . of employing but one centre and keeping it all within [the] hero's compass" (8, 9). If James's conception of this unity in diversity really operates, when we have completed *The Ambassadors*, we should be able to visualize the form of almost every action, detail, scene, and character of the novel all somehow "contained" within one center. This notion is similar to Emerson's idea that if we could know everything about a flower, we would know everything in the universe. The landing at Chester, Strether's discussions with Waymarsh and Maria Gostrey in the early scenes, and each incident thereafter, would be related ultimately to whatever is meant in the central speech in the garden—"Live all you can!"—not in literal detail but in a perception of idea, thought, and event with respect to the center.

Until now I have referred to the construction of "center" and "diverse parts" as if we were dealing with something a reader would appreciate only as an observer. I have been taking for granted a conception of fictional reality in which we, the readers, are "here" as observers, and the story, that spherical cluster of fibers around a core, is "there" as object. We assume that observer and object are separate and always remain so. But in Henry James, this is not the case. Over a period of years, James introduced a method that placed the reader in another location, as it were, so that he experiences the imaginary "spherical" shape from within. The reader both becomes a part of the diversity and at the same time remains at the center of everything.

The key, the "trick" of bringing off such a piece of magic, lies in the way the author develops a character's thoughts. Provided that we define thought satisfactorily, any action of a character, patterned as it is after the action of human beings, can be said to be preceded by some kind of thought, appearing in varying degrees of subtlety and intensity as one enters into the deeper recesses of the mind. Let us then define thought in James as a whole complex of activity, be it logic, emotion, day-dream, impulse, or reflex. Thus, by his ability to create and communicate the subtlest "thought" processes of a character, James perfected a type of story-telling that functions on a level beneath the surface activity of characters in the traditional novel. Percy Lubbock, in *The Craft of Fiction*, says that in James "the world of silent thought is thrown open, and thought itself becomes the vehicle by which the story is rendered." In dealing with a situation like Strether's, he says, James presents "the movement that flickers over the surface of [a character's] mind . . . the impulses and reactions of his mood [become] the players upon the new scene . . . we watch the thought itself, the hidden thing as it twists to and fro in his brain." As an alternative, the author could have stepped forward and explained the restless appearance of the character's thought, but James prefers the dramatic way. "The man's thought . . . can be made to reveal its [own] inwardness . . . " (157–58). The following is a minuscule example from *The Ambassadors* of the "hidden thing as it twists to and fro" (the book is filled with examples of Strether's inner mind at work, and indeed it is through the morphology of his collective thought that we best see the warp of his consciousness).

> What is clearest of all indeed was something much more than this, something at the single stroke of which—and wasn't it simply juxtaposition?—all vagueness vanished. It was the click of a spring—he saw the truth. He had by this time also met Chad's look; there was more of it in that; and the truth, accordingly, so far as Bilham's enquiry was concerned, had thrust in the answer. (139; 5, II)

That computer, Strether's brain, experiences a "single stroke"— possibly at bottom it is a "juxtaposition" of opposites or apparent opposites. By a stroke the vagueness vanishes. The stroke is like the click of a spring and the truth "thrusts in" an answer as if the inner brain were made up of electrical connections and other mechanisms. The strokes and clicks end up with what could for all intents and purposes be a robotic arm feeding in the final clue to produce the outcome. Such terms are simply dramatizing thought itself: first, the traditional novel did not concern itself primarily with thought, and, second, dramatization is the quickest way for others to experience, to be, a subject. Thus, in a detached sense, the reader becomes part of the diversity of his thought. It remains to demonstrate as we go along how he becomes part of Strether's change as a whole.

As MacLuhan might say, the thought of the hero is the medium. But also, the thoughts of the hero are at the center of the action, since the action consists of the consciousness of successive details of a character's world. Finally, in *The Ambassadors*, the hero's thoughts are the *only* ones we are allowed to know completely. How then can we know the thoughts of characters other than the hero? We know them only partially by his interpretation of them, by his conjecture and his observation—which give us the illusion that we actually know other characters' thoughts. The process, though to an extent illusion, becomes convincing, as we shall see.

In the following passage, Strether, having met Madame de Vionnet (the woman suspected of corrupting his young friend) in Notre Dame Cathedral, mentions that he has just purchased several volumes of Victor Hugo: then he waits impatiently for an answer.

> She however took her time; she drew out their quiet gossip as if she had wished to profit by their meeting, and this confirmed precisely an interpretation of her manner, of her mystery. While she rose, as he would have called it, to the question of Victor Hugo, her voice itself, the light low quaver of her deference to the solemnity about them, seemed to make her words mean something that they didn't mean openly. Help, strength, peace, a sublime support—she hadn't found so much of these things as the amount wouldn't be sensibly greater for any scrap his appearance of faith in her might enable her to feel in her hand. (183; 7, I)

Understandably, one could read this passage for the first time and assume the lady is a person in need of help of a very sensitive and personal kind. Strether's subsequent thoughts are: "It was as to this he had made up his mind; he had made it up, that is, to give her a sign." Since clearly Strether plans to act on his diagnosis of her situation and help her, the reader can easily be swept along into accepting that she does feel she needs help. But, looking again, we notice that Strether only infers from her *manner* that she needs this help, and from the "light low quaver" . . . that "seemed to make her words mean something that they didn't mean openly." There is nothing but circumstantial evidence presented to us, through observed detail, that she is *in fact* in need of help. And one can go through other passages in the novel testing the evidence and find that other characters think or feel for the most part what Strether attributes to them. At the same time, given the imaginative and intimate revelations of his mind, if we accept his judgment, we find we have a convincing story to follow.

What we have been describing, prior to and in this passage, are two separate components of the novel that now come together as one: first, the principle governing the content of the novel, James's "compositional law," wherein all diversity is contained in one center; second, the principle governing the moment-by-moment action of the novel wherein the author draws the reader's mind into the center of the content by taking him into the processes of the hero's mind. But the hero's mind, since it is mainly his thoughts we really know, is in that sense the content of the novel. Thus, the technical instrument portraying the content is the same "creature" as the content itself.

A little farther on in the Preface, James asserts that this center has an "absoluteness" about it. He does so as follows: in referring to the "germ" that contains all things, he mentions another garden, another house of art, where these few words were first spoken (2). This is the actual event, the actual place where his friend W. D. Howells spoke similar words to the artist, Jonathan Sturges, and prompted what later became James's seminal idea for *The Ambassadors*. In this earlier setting, on a summer afternoon, the many interesting persons who were there, and everything else, combined to give the scene what he calls a "note absolute." In it he recognized "on the spot" the greater part of his purpose. It had been driven in with hard taps, "like some stake from the noose of a cable." Round about it there was a "swirl of current" that characterized the rest of the "time and place and scene." Again the principle appears: stability in the midst of flux, rushing waters of changeability round an absolute center. "All the elements of a situation most to my taste were there . . . we must for the time . . . at least figure its merit and its dignity as *possibly* absolute. What it comes to . . . is that even among the supremely good . . . there is an ideal *beauty* of goodness the invoked action of which is to raise the artistic faith to its maximum" (2).

The conception has a strong hint of Platonism, both in the notion of a transcendent good and in the equation of beauty and goodness. He is saying that, with reference to *The Ambassadors*, our center now takes on an ideal value which, when achieved, lies beyond the flow of everything "relative" or ephemeral: there is a quality of "supreme goodness" in the supremely good, and within it an ideal "*beauty* of goodness." When the supremely good perceive the ideal invoked in the actual, they "raise the artistic faith" to its supreme, its *absolute* capacity.

In point of fact, the speech in the Fifth Book comprising the "note absolute" *is* struck in the midst of a new perspective Strether has gained just moments before. Thus, the tiny center does evoke something of the principles James speaks of—it evokes a higher, transcendent reality. I am referring to two scenes, one in which Strether meets Gloriani (5, I), and another immediately following (5, II), in which he meets Mme. de Vionnet.

The garden of the great artist was a place, the novel says, "as striking . . . as a treasure dug up." In the background, the bird-haunted trees, the high party-walls, the grave hotels stood off for privacy spoke "a strong, indifferent persistent order." The distinguished sculptor, with a single look at Strether, affected him as a "dazzling prodigy of type." He had come in midcareer from his native Rome to Paris

> . . . where *with a personal lustre almost violent, he shone in con-*
> *stellation: all of which was more than enough to crown him, for his*
> *guest, with the light, with the romance of glory.* Strether, in contact
> with that element as he had never yet so intimately been, *had the*
> *consciousness of opening to it, for the happy instant, all the windows of*
> *his mind, of letting this rather grey interior drink in for once the sun of*
> *a clime not marked in his old geography.* He was to remember again
> repeatedly the medal-like Italian face, in which every line was an
> artist's own, in which time told only as tone and consecration;
> and he was to recall in especial, *as the penetrating radiance, as the*
> *communication of the illustrious spirit itself,* the manner in which,
> while they stood briefly, in welcome and response, face to face, he
> was held by the sculptor's eyes. He wasn't soon to forget them,
> was to think of them, all unconscious, untending, preoccupied
> though they were, as *the source of the deepest intellectual sounding*
> *to which he had ever been exposed.* (124–25; 5, I; italics mine)

Strether has had all along a redeeming trait, the trait of openmindedness, so he *can* learn. The result is that he undergoes a particularly significant learning process now, the completion of which he is yet only dimly aware, even though that awareness is potentially within himself. In the scene, he has taken another step toward the core at the depths of that "sphere"—toward something "supremely good"; it is a level of awareness that supercedes all the other levels he has known up to this point in his life.

In the scene, Gloriani and Strether exchange not a single word. Strether's experience is impersonal because Gloriani is an abstraction, not a character designed to become involved in any way other than to radiate his silent influence on Strether, like a god descending to prepare Strether for the more personal moments in store for him with Marie de Vionnet and then the moments involving the rest of his life. Gloriani is the underlying (or overarching) light of "Paris" or "Europe" that shines through everything and illuminates the "new" universe in its most abstract sense. Strether at the moment readily perceives the light that is there, the "deepest intellectual sounding," and appreciates it without yet surrendering to anything beyond the first impression.

The scene next in store for Strether is pictured, in the full text surrounding the "few words," by means of a lavishly beautiful flow of impressions on the mind. At first, the splendor of it all holds his attention; then Mme. de Vionnet appears. He starts a conversation with her, but she is suddenly pulled away by another guest who uses "a trick . . . three words" with a social art of which Strether is no master.

Just then the rush of impressions in the garden stops. "He sat there alone for five minutes, with plenty to think of: above all with the sense of having been dropped by a charming woman *overlaid more by other impressions and in fact quite cleared and different*. He hadn't *yet had so quiet a surrender*; he didn't in the least care if nobody spoke to him more" (136; 5, II; italics mine).

He goes through a series of steps in these two scenes. First, he studies the garden ("Paris"), taking in new impressions. Then Gloriani's entrance causes him to collect his various impressions and a second stage occurs, a deep *intellectual* sounding, the deepest of his life. He has opened his vision to some vague apparition of Paris—the Paris that is idea, not fact. After some conversation and a change of scene, he focuses on Marie, and then she abruptly departs from him. Had this departure upset him? Is that what happened? Is that why he looks "floored"? The answer is no. "If he had been overturned at all," he says, "he had been overturned into the upper air, the sublime element with which he had an affinity, and in which he might be trusted awhile to float."

During the whole experience, from beginning to end, his thoughts shift from one avenue of perception to another as if they were spiralling "downward" in his mind, reaching successive glimpses of objects, shapes, and forms that he is directed toward by the still overpowering light of the great artist. As he marvels at the newness of things, he finds an excitement, an explosion of feeling, and a growing insight. After he has met Marie, he speaks suddenly of having seen "an immensity." Bilham offers to introduce him to more friends. Strether refuses. He is quite content as he is, wants to talk to no one, "having nothing to say and finding it [the scene] would do beautifully as it was . . . . "

We have seen first, then, the rushing currents of diversity followed by the "light" of Gloriani (a preparation for Marie). Next comes his personal contact with the consciousness of Marie followed by her departure, sending or overturning him into the "sublime element." Finally, there is the halting of the rushing currents brought on by his "quiet surrender." Each step has moved him closer to the core, the stable element of his own consciousness. From the multitude of sound around him has come silence; from diversity has come unity.

Now he strikes the note. *Now* he makes his speech, because at this moment the most important insight of his life is forced to the surface. *However*, in order to overflow with the declaration that one must "live all [one] can," as he does, he needs some awareness of what it means to do so, and what happens in this moment of silence after Marie's departure represents the first inkling he has had of it.

He has done several important things: he has surrendered his control; he has surrendered to some sublime element; he has surrendered by means of silence—a silence that he has always been capable of but he has never experienced in this way until now. His surrender has brought: unity. It is more or less his beginning. His first reaction to his own advice is that it is all over for him, "too late." Of course! This is to be expected! It is rather, in fact, too *soon* to break a habit of forty or fifty years during which he has always looked upon things as impossible, never to be enjoyed, risky, expensive, or simply inappropriate, and to decide suddenly that they are all something entirely different from what he has thought. And so he doesn't accept the new experience for what it is. But he has had a glimpse that tells him something different is here. An exclamation suddenly springs out of him: "Oh I do see; and more than you'd believe or I can express"—this happens before he drops back, momentarily, into his old pattern of doubt, hesitancy, and negativity.[1]

These passages form the center of the most crucial scenes in *The Ambassadors*. The later scene is a microcosm in several brushstrokes of all the thousands of brushstrokes in the full portrait. Apart from whatever ensuing good, bad, or mixed relationships Strether has with other characters, the fundamental motif of the drama is rooted in the *sort* of change the hero's mind begins to undergo

---

[1] See Appendix to this book for a further look at the substance of "things never dreamt of" by Strether.

here. It consists of an exposure of his own "Woollett philosophy" to the "Paris philosophy" inspired by the god, Gloriani, and the new "incarnation," Marie de Vionnet. These last two are catalytic to a mind in pursuit of *itself*. By being exposed to the "Paris philosophy," Strether is exposed to a core of truth *already present* in his mind as he follows his journey of self-exploration. From this point on we will be concerned with that journey.

In the Preface, James tells us what transpires on a layer beneath the surface of the plot to retrieve Chad from a life of sin. He says Strether arrives at the Paris garden in a "false position," bound by "narrow localism." He has a "moral scheme of the most approved pattern . . . yet framed to break down on any approach to vivid facts . . . . " This warns us that the breaking down of Strether has nothing to do with the traditional tempted state of visitors to Paris: " . . . these inductive steps" that change the position such as the view he has of Marie and subsequently of Chad "could only be as rapid as they were distinct . . . he was . . . literally undergoing . . . a change from hour to hour" (6). Once the original false moral position—which James himself calls "the philosophy of Woollett"—has been dissolved, things "that have never been dreamt of in [that] philosophy" can take its place.

But what has never been dreamt of? To answer this we must return to that speech where Strether declares one must live all he can. What does he mean by "live"? He seems not to mean the quantity of experience, as if to say, "To have lived you must have a great deal of that particular experience." Nor is he saying that we must have one *kind* of experience only, such as sex, or passionate love, or adventure, or suffering, or joy, or whatever, because living will, to different persons, consist of different combinations of these.

He seems to mean the quality of experience. But this poses still another problem. Two people might have exactly the same experience, yet would rate it differently. The solution to the problem must be that what makes one experience differ in quality from another is something one brings to the experience: i.e., one's "awareness."

Finally, if we were to define the term as Strether uses it in his speech, would it still have the same meaning for him at the end of the novel? Just as he himself undergoes a change, Strether's idea of what it means to live may also undergo a change. I want to address all these speculations, partly with some responses already made by others, partly with some new responses.

In his central "few words" speech, Strether claims that he himself hasn't lived at all. He gives the reason that for him it is too late: "It's as if the train had fairly waited at the station for me without my having had the gumption to know it was there. Now I hear its faint receding whistle miles and miles down the line" (137; 5, II).

The Ambassadors is about a man who, as he grows older, thinks he has missed his life. In other words, it is about a great many people on earth. For one who does reach a point of feeling he hasn't lived, is it a temporary or a permanent feeling? Take Strether. He has just recently focused his attention on an attractive and sophisticated woman in a world of such rich sights and sounds as Paris, and he has also focused his attention on a close friend newly transformed into an interesting and sophisticated young man. Within a few minutes after he finishes his key speech, he reflects that he would like to have been Chad. Both he and Chad came from New England, yet Chad miraculously broke free of its conventional restraints and found himself happily oriented to the freedom of Europe and all that that implies, including being in love with an alluring countess.

One can understand how Strether feels! Yet one also sees how what he believes with all his heart about missing life could change in later years. After all, in spite of his age, what had seemed a limited and wasted existence could transform in his memory into a preparation for a fuller life and far greater happiness than he had ever dreamed possible.[2]

In his notebook entry of October 28, 1895, James himself gives us some clues about what "living" could mean to Strether. It could mean, he says, experiencing "sensations, passions, impulses, pleasures . . . in the presence of some great human spectacle, some great experiment and perception, for Enjoyment, in a word [to become], sur la fin, or toward it, sorrowfully aware" (Notebooks 66; latter emphasis mine). In focusing on the completed work, Leon Edel discovers a further and even more precise indication of what Strether could mean by "living":

> The novel he wrote about his middle-aged hero had a single
> primary message, for himself as for his readers: that one must live

---

[2] "If the nub of Einstein's Special Relativity can be considered as resting within any one sentence, it rests in the realization that one man's 'now' is another man's 'then'; now itself is a subjective conception, valid only for an observer with one special frame of reference" (Clark 88). See also p. 39 of this chapter where this statement is used in another context.

in full awareness and 'with sufficient intensity' to be a source of 'what may be called excitement to oneself.' (*Master* 70)

There is strong consensus, in other words, that living is awareness. Let us pursue this idea. There are two clearly different states that Strether experiences in the novel. In the beginning we see his cloudy, awkward early mental and emotional condition, shrouded as it is in his "New England conscience," but at the end he exhibits a sharp, clear, discriminating mind. In the early stage, he simply "is"; in the late one, he both "is" and "is aware." The difference between the two conditions in him is extreme enough so that one can almost speak of two Strethers, or at least two distinct states of consciousness in Strether. In the early scene with Maria Gostrey at Chester (Book 2), Strether tells her that he thinks knowing he comes from a place like Woollett is to know "the worst": ("It sticks out of me"). He's afraid of her finding him "too hopeless" and a failure, a failure which is part of Woollett's failure in general. Gostrey pushes his confession further: "The failure to enjoy[?]"; he admits this, and as if that weren't enough he ends by remarking directly to her [though he is *supposed* to be joking]: "I'm afraid of you!"

The novel's beginning shows a man who feels inadequacy; hopelessness; personal failure (plus the inability to enjoy life); and insecurity bordering on fear, particularly fear of women. In the end, he is much loved by his friends. He tries to improve the quality of their lives rather than trying, as before, to manipulate them. In the beginning, he had to grope to find his identity in others; at the end, others look to him for advice and direction. At the end, he finally begins to see the whole, the entire picture—the couple he has come out to chastise, Chad with his limitations, and Marie with, in addition to her limitations, all her "fineness" and "subtlety" (342; 12, II). He had seen Marie through the eyes of Chad because his early friendship for Chad had given him enough faith in the young man's taste and good sense to enable him to do this, and because in those days he was dependent almost entirely on others for navigation. But he is not Chad, and in fact he has tremendous imagination and discrimination of his own. When he "gets there," where Chad has been (in that final scene in Marie's apartment) as close to her as Chad was, he is able to go beyond the view that Chad's eyes, highly developed but still limited, "only mortal," afforded him. What he sees is the subject of this "[once] vicarious"[3] joy. He had caught a

---

[3] This phrase comes from James's "Project of Novel" (*Notebooks* 370).

flash of the "essential" Marie when he first met her at Gloriani's. Now, when he sees her for the last time, and knows all, the sexual liaison, the deceptions about it, he feels still the same as he did when he had had that prevision of something extra-ordinary about her in Gloriani's garden—only now he recognizes and understands her much more personally, and

> once more, and yet once more, he could trust her. That is he could trust her to make deception right. As she presented things the ugliness—goodness knew why—went out of them. (337; 12, I)

He has surrendered to something a little bit beyond the evidence, and the capability of such a surrender says a great deal about what he has become. Whatever else he does, at this moment Strether has crossed a line, as if he had (again, but this time more fully) transcended the circumference of the "sphere" of fibers around a central core visualized earlier. A great deal of this transcendence involves awareness, but there is more to it than that. The earlier Strether was not capable of the freedom he experiences now; in no way would he attempt to manipulate her now as had been his original plan. He would want her needs to come to fruition as much as he would want his own. He cultivates this growth in her on the basis of the confidence that he has nothing to fear by doing so.

In his "Project of Novel" just noted, Henry James refers to the dramatic shift in Strether's thinking, which culminates in the scene described here, as a *"volte face"* (*Notebooks* 227). Let us characterize this event in terms of another discipline as a means of indicating further the wider implications of what James has embodied in this moment of change. Thomas Kuhn, in *The Structure of Scientific Revolutions*, denotes the basic theoretical model underlying the main body of a science as a "paradigm." Similarly, different types of mental experience involve different models. And indeed, one fundamental frame of reference underlies and conditions all experience: our sense of identity. For example, children of a certain age still react to the world with an "I" versus "it" model: "me-in-here" versus "world-out-there." One takes from "out there" to feed "in here," and so forth. The child needs this distinction to affirm his personal identity, and this duality builds up a model that carries over into adult years. But the experience that most shakes this model is the experience of a unity with the rest of creation. Once the individual realizes, not just understands intellectually, his own consciousness as inseparable from the world "out there," and once he *sees* that such an approach cannot be incorporated into the old model, he starts shifting to a new model. Therein begins the new sense of identity comparable to the shift that a civilization undergoes when it changes its perception of reality, as when man changes (and is still changing) his perspective based on Newton's reality to the reality of Einstein. It is indeed a *volte face*. And as we go into these examples, it becomes clear that while the change is not limited to the "visual," yet the visual change, in the sense of its designating the way he perceives things, however intangible, is fundamental. The change takes Strether from:

1.	self-centeredness	to	selflessness
2.	"unsureness," inadequacy, self-doubt	to	"sureness," confidence, self-assurance
3.	fear	to	courage
4.	rigidity	to	flexibility
5.	lack of enjoyment	to	enjoyment
6.	dependence on others	to	independence but not aloofness
7.	possessiveness in relationships	to	a trusting, "let live" approach
8.	living by the clock	to	living "timelessly"
9.	a puritanical view of experience as moral abstraction	to	a "European" view of experience based on the senses
10.	life viewed through the mind as doctrine	to	life viewed through the freedom of the imagination
11.	a commercial, materialistic outlook—the "Woollett" approach	to	a "European" appreciation of art, beauty
12.	ignorance, "darkness"	to	knowledge, light

In mentioning these characteristics, I wish to emphasize the direction of the change before anything else. In general, Strether can be said to move from a limited to an unlimited state of consciousness. His early consciousness is "closed," and the late one is "open." For instance, R. W. Stallman elaborates on No. 8 above (from a "puritanical view" to a "European view") and No. 9 ("living by the clock" vs. living "timelessly"). He sees an expansion from a limited to an unlimited conception of time in Strether's consciousness. He distinguishes the "Woollett" side of Strether, which locks him into an adherence to time, from the

"Paris" side, which is timeless. The Woollett side is reluctant to "live time" except by the clock: "everyone from Woollett has his mind made up; they all live by what is predictable, conventional, preconceived." Strether gradually opens himself to a recognition of what it means to "live in the Now." To explain this, Stallman quotes James on the later Strether: "Everything he wanted was comprised in a single boon: the common, unattainable art of taking things as they came." Or, as Strether himself says later: "It's the impulse to let things be." "There are times," Stallman concludes, "when, as it were, the clock stops and the pendulum of [his] mind halts for moments of enjoyment . . . moments of passive perception [which] constitute for Strether his happiest occasions."

Robert E. Long discusses three of the characteristics on this list (9, 10, and 11) in an illuminating article. These three also exhibit that movement I have described as going from limited to limitless consciousness. To Long, Strether's early state of mind is characterized by "suppression of the imagination." He says the loss of his wife produced in Strether a form of renunciation of the life of the emotions. It was his contact with Europe that re-excited his imagination. Strether's hesitations and renunciations are, historically speaking, a "cultural residue of the Puritan suspicion of the flesh and of worldliness." He notes the tendency of New England Protestantism to react instinctively to experience as a moral abstraction (compare to Strether's "false moral position" discussed in this chapter, p. 30), and constructs an opposition of mind—that is, whatever is of "New England and puritan"—and imagination—that is, what constitutes "Europe, art, and the freedom thereof."

This is the opposition between authoritarian puritanism—associated not only with mind but also with law and moral order—and an imaginative inventiveness that Strether discovers in sense experience. Thus, he undergoes another widening of his perspective: from conformity with external definitions of experience to relying on his own ingenuity; from suppressed to free emotion; from fear of "the flesh" to a trust in his own observations based on one-to-one contact with life; and from an overdependence on law or duty and moral order to reliance on acts that are spontaneous. In other words, he has undergone a whole series of changes, all of which move him from limited to limitless awareness.

In the opposing concepts above (p. 34, No. 12), images of light successively illustrate the development of Strether's awareness. Three striking examples of that imagery can be identified in *The*

Ambassadors. The first, occurring in the scene in the Luxembourg Gardens (60; 2, II), begins by contrasting the splendor Strether sees in the gardens with the all-too-familiar discouraging past that still haunts him. He starts by dwelling on how he has failed in everything, been unwittingly selfish, and "done so much for so little," and goes on with how "he hadn't had the gift of making the *most* of what he had" (63). But under the garden's spell, he suddenly feels like spring, like the morning breeze, like becoming free: "Buried for long years in dark corners . . . these few germs had sprouted again under forty-eight hours of Paris" (64). Thus, through the cloud of his self-renunciation he has found himself nearly accepting himself as part of the new place, the garden:

> His greatest uneasiness seemed to peep at him out of the imminent impression that almost any acceptance of Paris might give one's authority away. It hung before him this morning, this vast bright Babylon, like some huge iridescent object, a jewel brilliant and hard, in which parts were not to be discriminated and differences comfortably marked. It twinkled and trembled and melted together, and what seemed all surface one moment seemed all depth the next. (66; 2, II)

He reacts to this vision with his characteristic former "double consciousness," the one part regressing toward Woollett, the other looking ahead, embracing Paris, but the two hopelessly separated. The parts "not to be discriminated" and "melting together" give him an unrestrained enjoyment, which, because unfamiliar, is frightening; at the same time, the "parts not to be discriminated" do comprise the substance of everything that is *not* Woollett, *not* fearful, *not* failure-ridden, whatever is not familiar to him as part of the old order and therefore more stable than ever. The brilliantly hard light of the jewel is beginning to replace the dark past.

He has again obtained a preliminary glimpse of the "source," the "core," of the sphere of his universe. As soon as he finds himself tempted to accept that universe, his "Paris" and (with trepidation) the "Babylonian" aspect of it, its brilliance, and maybe even its pleasure (!)—he falters, and starts to wonder whether it is possible to like it some, without liking it too much. He ends up finding the garden "incontestably adorable," and—well, as for "taking it," he says he would "do what he reasonably could." Thus in terms of a conscious commitment, Strether has made a step, albeit a timid one.

In the second phase, the imagery of radiant light in Gloriani's garden reinforces and deepens the impressions of Paris begun at the Luxembourg. He says that, somewhere within the mixed elements around him in that garden, not obvious, but buried, not something he would be able to overcome by forethought, but unexpectedly, unpredictably, he detects—something. A feeling? An intuition? Whatever it is, it has, as we noted before, a "strong, indifferent, persistent order." Given the many possible interpretations of this phrase, one idea it certainly conveys is *stability*. He also gets the sense of "a great convent, a convent of missions . . . a nursery of young priests, of scattered shade, straight alleys, and chapel-bells." Again, whatever else it represents, his imagery conveys an ordered, protected peace. Close upon this follows the passage about the sunlight that I have quoted more fully earlier. Here I want to focus on just one section of it:

> Strether, in contact with that element as he had never yet so intimately been, had the consciousness of opening to it, for the happy instant, all the windows of his mind, of letting his grey interior drink in for once the sun of a clime not marked in his old geography. (125; 5, I)

He says of course that he has never experienced this sort of thing (this particular kind of sunlight) before, and he opens his entire mind to receive it. The experience strikes him as a happy one ("good," "enjoyable"). In fact, he drinks in the light of the star (or sun) of the constellation, and *this* reveals to him a new area of life, uncharted, one that transcends what preceded it, as is evident when James calls it "the source of the deepest intellectual sounding to which he had ever been exposed."

Now we come to the third and main part, the part that echoes what Henry James speaks of in the Preface in referring to unity and diversity, absolute and relative. This light has two separate and distinct degrees of brightness. The first is new—the central light, the sun, the star of the constellation, the "source." The second, consisting of those rays familiar to Strether in his old geography, opposes this. The image in his mind distinguishes between a relative and an absolute light, or between a complete, pure light, and a partial, incomplete one which has mere degrees of brightness. Both of these types of light can be found in the Luxembourg image—the mixed being the discriminated light and opposite to it the "melted" or "undiscriminated" one. In both cases, here and in the Luxembourg, we have *limited* (shadowed, fluctuating, incomplete) light and a *limitless* (pure, stable, complete)[4] one. The latter transcends the everyday level of "brightness." It might be called an ideal brightness. This is the level Strether had never experienced in his old geography—central, uncharted, unpredictable, *enjoyable*, the source of his deepest intellectual sounding. The two kinds of light correspond to "Woollett," the conventional, and "Paris," the ideal, or "free" form of Strether's thought.

The kind of individual change occurring in Strether corresponds to the change from the notion of time and space as constants as it occurred to Newton to the gradual reliance on the notion of Einstein, to whom time and space are constantly changing. All this took over half a century to come about. In his Special Theory of Relativity, Einstein tells us that the velocity of light never changes, whereas time, as well as distance (or space, in the sense of its being measured distance), are constantly changing, and are not, as Newtonian principles urged, constant and "absolute." To explain the Einsteinian theory, R. W. Clark constructs a simple illustration. He asks us to imagine a sailor standing on the deck of a ship as it sails parallel to a long jetty. At each end of the jetty stands a signal lamp. Midway between the two lamps stands an observer:

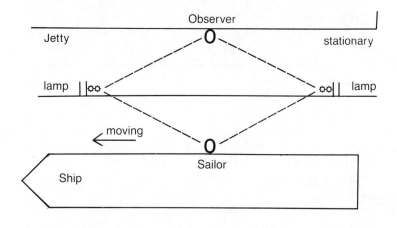

----

[4] The terms "stable" and "complete" are used because of the expressions "not to be discriminated" and "melted"—used in the image, implying that the parts have been melted or reduced to their most fundamental condition—a "ground state" as the term is used in modern physics. The parts or "particles" of this state are described by physicists as being "undifferentiated" or "undiscriminated." The same is true of William James's "pure experience." (See Chapter I, p. 15.)

At the precise moment the sailor passes the observer, flashes of light are sent out by the two lamps; they are perceived by both sailor and observer. So far as the stationary observer is concerned, the light rays are sent from both directions at exactly the same time. The light rays coming from each end of the jetty have to travel the same distance to reach him, and they will reach him simultaneously. So far, so good. But what about the sailor on the ship—who will have been at an equal distance from both lamps as each sent out its light signal? He knows that both flashes travel with the same speed. Although this speed is very great, it is finite, and since he is moving away from one lamp and toward the other he will receive light signals at different times from the observer on the jetty. As far as he is concerned, the lamps will not have been switched on simultaneously.

Remember, (1) the observer is midway between the lamps, (2) the lamps flash simultaneously (as long as there is no motion on the part of either participant), and (3) they flash at the moment the sailor is precisely opposite the observer. When the final part of the experiment is performed, the only difference in the whole situation will be that the sailor's ship will be moving. This factor will change the perception the two men have of the speed of the light rays.

Supposing one of the men wished to recheck the conditions of the experiment. First he would measure the time it takes the light rays to reach the location of each man, and then the space (or distance) of each man from the lamps. In Newton's terms, in whatever situation one measures them, their dimensions will be the same. The Einstein experiment overthrew this notion. As mentioned before, "one man's 'now' becomes another man's 'then'; 'now' [became] a subjective conception, valid only for an observer within one specific frame of reference." (Clark 88). In short, perceptions of time and space are relative.

But if they are relative, what are they relative to? Or, to put this more urgently: "Prior to Einstein's theory, the way we measured time and space constituted the basis of everything we knew in the physical universe. Without such a basis, would not the result be chaos?"

Einstein provided an answer. The one thing that is constant in the physical universe is the speed of light, which is a "maximum in the electromagnetic and the mechanical worlds." Light travels with a velocity that is independent of the bodies emitting or receiving it.

The new theory has broader implications. Assuming our think-ing consists of abstract patterns that build from such elemental phys-ical perceptions, which it does, the new theory changed the basis of our thinking. Society assimilates the ramifications of such a change slowly, but eventually man's thought in the new society is differ-ent in that his awareness (due to clearer perception) has immensely expanded. He has established a new order, a new "geography."

Assume that Strether, educated at a time when Newtonian physics dominated every conception of society, Strether, a citizen of Woollett, with a "Woollett" perspective has been observing the whole experiment. He is given full cognizance of all the measurements with the ship standing still and again with the ship in motion. He is puzzled at the discrepancy in the perceptions of the speed of the light rays. Enter Einstein—a citizen of Paris with a "Paris" perspective. Einstein shows him how the old measurements of time and space are void and that the proper yardstick is the speed of light.

The analogy only goes so far, because for Strether to reach the second stage and become a citizen of Paris, throughout his whole perception, as in the novel, something has to develop within him and become permanent that is not an intellectual construct or belief, but something so natural as to be automatic, something that functions in him even though he cannot see or control it, like an internal bodily organ. In the experiment, the constant speed of light corresponds to a stable component, the core, the central light discussed in the light passages in the text of The Ambassadors. Once Strether has found that core, all the remaining "currents," like the perceptions of time and space in the Einstein analogy, can fluctuate and there will still be internal rest and order to which these changing things can be related as to a base. He will be established in the unity of his own awareness, with a new, more secure and far-reaching perspective of the diversity it encompasses. He will have undergone a human shift like the paradigm shift. He has transcended the old reality and become integrated with a new, higher reality. All this Strether has begun to establish quite naturally and spontaneously in Gloriani's garden.

The change in Strether is similar to the one we ourselves undergo if we observe the experiment described above and permit our minds to depart from space and time as our referents, recognizing a new one in the speed of light. But the difference between our experience and Strether's would be that ours is the product of external physical perception, while Strether's results from a discovery in his inner mind.

How does the stable referent he encounters affect him? In Book 10, Strether is under attack from Sarah Pocock for having turned his back on Mrs. Newsome and Woollett and gone over to the enemy. The scene contrasts the rage of Sarah, who has been appointed to the office of avenging angel by Mrs. Newsome, with the new consciousness of Strether, who is now wiser and more confident than ever. In the scene, Sarah is in a blind fury, insulting, threatening, and viciously attacking her old friend. At this moment she positively loathes everything Strether stands for. She asks this question:

> You can sacrifice mothers and sisters to her [Marie] without a blush, and can make them cross the ocean on purpose to feel the more and take from you [all] the straighter, *how* do you do it?

Strether's reply to her clarifies what I mean by "stable referent" in the midst of diversity:

> I don't think there's anything I've done in any such calculated way as you describe. Everything has come as a sort of indistinguishable part of everything else. Your coming out belonged closely to my having come before you, and my having come was the result of our general state of mind. Our general state of mind had proceeded, on its side, from our queer ignorance, our queer misconceptions and confusions—from which, since then, *an inexorable tide of light* seems to have floated us into our perhaps still queerer knowledge. (293; 10, III; emphasis mine)

This passage contains James's third image of light. The first was that in the Luxembourg; the second was that in Gloriani's garden (see p. 27). And indeed, Strether's proclamation emerges with an "inexorable logic." Nothing has been done in Strether's universe by calculated design, but spontaneously, by a natural evolution of things, springing from a harmony of the universe. From his shaky and insecure beginning, Strether now sees that it all fits together. As he looks back he sees how he used to be confused, and indeed this new position, in the light of knowledge, *would* seem "queer"— calculated in design and queer in knowledge—to anyone in Sarah's fixed conventional framework of ideas. Again, in one sense, Strether can be seen as someone who has leapt ahead in history, departing from a world of Newtonian principles to arrive at Einstein's. In another sense the difference between his new position and Sarah's is very small. The same is true of Newton and Einstein.

Let me explain. The difference between the relative light flashes from the point of view of each individual in the illustration is so small as to make them almost imperceptible, a point that provoked one professor at the time of the discovery of special relativity to remark that, because we have no personal experience of the discrepancy in everyday life, our common sense revolts when we are asked to give up the old conceptions that result from it. This is very much like Sarah's situation. Strether understands very well why she and the interested parties in Woollett see things as they do because he can see their problems from his new vantage point *and from hers as well*. She, however, can only see from hers. She is frustrated and angry because he seems sinister in his attitude and utterly vicious in his treatment of Mrs. Newsome. On the other hand, he does not feel he has done anything wrong at all, nor does he in his understanding bear the slightest malice toward Mrs. Newsome or Sarah—even though her attack probably represents one of the most violent in James's writing. On the contrary, Strether sees "the interconnectedness of things"—with himself included in the tapestry—with remarkable composure, so much so that, knowing what it feels like to be part of things, yet not so much a part of them as to be obsessed with them, he remains compassionately self-sufficient, stable, and calm.

To Strether the concept of "inexorable" light points to a synthesis of the diversity of things, as simultaneously they "go back into" the core, the seed. Once again, his development can be pictured by a core surrounded by fibres growing out of it to form a sphere like a cortex around the core, the fibres every so often reaching beyond the edges of the whole sphere—of established boundaries—as if it were made up of Woollett-like convention. As the hero's consciousness grows, the fibres eventually transcend the boundaries. The hero is able to look out beyond them into absolute, infinite light. He sees no longer in a limited, but in a limitless way. Still, once he has broken out of the boundaries, he will nevertheless be able to look back on them and understand them, just as he understands Sarah in the midst of her anguish.

III

THE MODEL OF TRANSCENDENCE

In his "Project of Novel," written for the publisher of *The Ambassadors* in 1900, Henry James makes Lambert Strether experience "a kind of moral and intellectual drop or arrest—of the whole range of feeling that has kept him up hitherto"; and he says, "what has happened, through him, has really happened *for* him, for his own spirit, for his own queer sense of things, more than for any one or anything else" (*The Ambassadors* 387).

Two passages that might be the actual carrying out of such an expectation are to be found near the end of the novel. One appears at the beginning of the French countryside scene by the river; Strether looks back over his experiences in Paris and says that he "had a sense of success, of a finer harmony of things, nothing but what had turned out yet according to plan." The atmosphere was "relaxed"; peace "hung about him." He "lost himself anew" (in the Lambinet painting, to which he has been comparing the scene). It was "as if he had found out he was tired—tired not from his walk, but from that inward exercise which had known, on the whole, for three months, so little intermission. That was it—when once they were off he had dropped; this moreover was what he had dropped to, and now he was touching bottom" (321; 11, III).

In this passage, one could say Strether experiences a silence, an immobility, a sense of completion, and a harmony with nature or the environment.

Just following the French countryside scene, in a visit with Maria Gostrey, he thinks to himself thoughts I have pointed out before: "They [he and Maria] could trust the merciful elements to let them continue at peace . . . . It amused him that he might for all the world have been going to die . . . the scene was filled for him with so deep a death-bed hush, so melancholy a charm" (345–46; 12, III).

The second passage communicates an experience similar to the first, but adds something about a death that would be peaceful and fulfilling or else a "death" in life that would be much the same thing. The harmony with nature is reemphasized; he goes a bit further, however, to indicate the pleasantness and charm of the whole experience.[1] In general, both passages convey a *stopping* (or a slowing down to near stopping) *of the motion of the mind,* a slowing down to calmness or a lack of activity. After the second passage, he goes on to say that the present calm and motionless experience of "these caverns of Kubla Khan" will soon merge with Woollett, or "what would be, with everything there, changed for him." That, he says, will be the final revelation. It is not simply that he has been declaring his whole experience in Paris at an end here; he has characterized something entirely new that has happened to his mind. To use terms like "calm," "fulfillment," "bliss," "equanimity" is to *attempt* to capture what I will further define in this chapter. Finally, he knows there must be a synthesis of *this* condition (Paris) and the old mind (Woollett), and he says so (346; 12, III).[2]

---

[1] In the *Phaedo*, Plato describes an experience like the one Strether refers to. The true philosopher, searching for wisdom through purification of the soul, attempts to separate the soul as much as possible from the body and accustom it to withdrawing all contact with the body, concentrating on itself by itself. Since the soul and body are separated at death, Socrates calls this technique "practicing death." In physical death, the soul "goes away to a place that is, like itself, glorious, pure, and invisible—the true Hades or unseen world" (*Great Dialogues* 466ff).

Rhoda Orme-Johnson says: "It is clear from other dialogues that Socrates did not mean that one spent his time within thinking deeply, but that he was describing his methodology to lead the soul to an experience of absolute knowledge deeper than the usual level of intellectual inquiry" ("Doris Lessing").

[2] Rhoda Orme-Johnson describes an intriguingly similar situation: "An image that recurs frequently in myth and literature describes an individual's death-like descent into some dark, hidden place, such as the Underworld, and his return to the world of light at a higher level of psychic wholeness and power. Classic studies of this recurrent image such as Eliade's *Rites and Symbols of Initiation* or Campbell's *A Hero With a Thousand Faces* or Bodkin's *Archetypal*

Compare these passages with the moment after the first encounter of Strether and Marie at Gloriani's (125; 6, I). In that
scene, Strether's mind has a direction, a "motion," signaled in a fig-
urative way by the light imagery. Whatever *other* light there was in
Paris at the garden party, the light surrounding Gloriani ("crowning
him . . . with the romance of glory") was the most brilliant; it was
"the sun of a clime not marked in his old geography." It is that new,
"non-relative" light which absorbs him as a result of his moment of
silence following his encounter with Marie. It was a different light
ray altogether—one that transcended other, lesser rays to the extent
that he "had the consciousness of opening to it . . . all the windows
of his mind" (125; 5, I). The experience was one of reaching the
"base" or "absolute" of the Preface; that base was the germ from
which emerged the "live all you can" speech that followed his first
radiant experience. The "lesser" light, not in the immediate aura
of Gloriani, was diversified (the familiar light of the old geography) and embodied only the *promise* of the silence, order, clarity,
and peace of the brilliant newer light (the silence, etc., were there
before in Strether, but as yet latent, unmanifest).

Rhoda Orme-Johnson speaks on the subject of transcendence
in literature:

> Regardless of the approach, be it psychological realism or
> myth and symbol, the image of transcending lies at the heart of
> much literature. In fact, it seems that just as the actual experi-
> ence of transcending transforms human life and leads it in the
> direction of psychic wholeness and integration, so the symbolic
> transcendence that occurs in imaginative literature seems to be
> necessary for the full development of its hero, and may, in fact,
> promote the expansion of his reader's consciousness. Through the
> experience of the work of art . . . the reader is thrown back into
> the self, led inwardly to increasingly refined and more joyful lay-
> ers of consciousness, and then transformed into a fuller, more
> integrated individual. (*Handbook* 128)

As we move forward from Gloriani's garden, minute by minute
Strether's consciousness is making the promise symbolized by the

---

Patterns in Poetry all describe the symbolic death and rebirth of the hero as
crucial to full human development."
She continues: "The imagery probably arises because it describes the natural
movement of consciousness inward toward the source of thought and creativity.
In fact, the most fundamental law of nature operative in the mind may be that
which describes transcending the surface level of thinking activity to subtler,
more holistic levels of thought and feeling" (*Handbook* 20).

light imagery a reality. Another way to say it is that he is in the act of moving from "surface" level to "depth" level consciousness. He does this in repeated patterns, that is, dips into the Second Level (depth level) then returns to the surface afterwards.

The condition Strether finds himself in at the end, indicated in the previous quotations, is then a transcendent state of consciousness, and he is just at the beginning of integrating the two, the original "ordinary" and the transcendental "extra-ordinary." I am assuming here, as does William James, that consciousness is a flow of images, ideas, feelings, thought, reflexes and other experiences in the mind.[3] When a person is awake and going about his business, consciousness is active and appears to be forward-moving or flowing; at least, this is the way Joyce and others have depicted it in their writings—as a flow. The following quotation from *Ulysses* is part of Molly Bloom's now famous "flow" of consciousness. The interesting aspect of this paragraph is that it shows the flow mainly of silent moments. Most of what she says are things she probably seldom talks about, but in showing them to us Joyce shows us one of the tenderest and most loving aspects of the person:

> . . . who was the first person in the universe before there was anybody that made it all who ah they dont know that they dont know neither do I so there you are they might as well try to stop the sun from rising tomorrow the sun shines for you he said the day we were lying among the rhododendrons on Howth head in the grey tweed suit and his straw hat the day I got him to propose to me yes first I gave him a bit of seedcake out of my mouth and it was leapyear like now yes 16 years ago my God after that long kiss I nearly lost my breath yes he said I was a flower of the mountain yes so we are flowers all a womans body yes that was one true thing he said in his life and the sun shines for you today yes that was why I liked him because I saw he understood or felt what a woman is. (282)

In *The Common Reader*, Virginia Woolf gives us a description of consciousness and explains the way a fiction writer could portray it. Her description amounts to what is ultimately a flow, but it also has two other features: it indicates a capacity of consciousness to grow, and it hints that the "inner" consciousness has a direct connection

---

[3] Transcendental consciousness, or "pure" consciousness, or "pure experience" in William's terminology, is, philosophically speaking, pure "being." When "being" becomes more active, when being becomes "doing," then consciousness becomes a flow of images, ideas, etc.

with "outer" consciousness—the environment or something beyond
that—as "atoms fall upon the mind."

> Examine for a moment an ordinary mind on an ordinary day. The
> mind receives a myriad impressions—trivial, fantastic, evanes-
> cent, or engraved with the sharpness of steel. From all sides they
> come, an incessant shower of innumerable atoms; and as they
> fall, as they shape themselves into the life of Monday or Tuesday,
> the accent falls differently from of old . . . . Life is not a series
> of gig lamps symmetrically arranged; life is a luminous halo, a
> semi-transparent envelope surrounding us from the beginning of
> consciousness to the end . . . . Let us record the atoms as they fall
> upon the mind in the order in which they fall, let us trace the pat-
> tern, however disconnected and incoherent in appearance, which
> each sight or incident scores upon the consciousness. (154–55)

Henry James's depiction is also a flow, but he does not try to
represent it by merely quoting the thoughts—as the inner mind
in motion—of the character (though he does that, too). Often he
stands outside and insinuates himself into the thoughts of the character. Thus he allows the character to observe, report, interpret, be
interrupted by, remembered events—or have another consciousness
enter and contribute to the flow. All these methods are technical instruments. What they produce, or a combination of them produces,
is a depth of feeling, or opinion, or prejudice, or hatred, or self-
hatred, or affectation, or affection—whatever the scene demands.
The depth, or penetration, appears everywhere. Some of it appears
in a random sample of Mrs. Gereth's consciousness in *The Spoils of
Poynton*. In this case the author enters and becomes the mind of
the character, who happens to be Mrs. Gereth:

> She prepared in her room for the little rural walk, and on her way
> down again, passing through corridors and observing imbecilities
> of decoration, the aesthetic misery of the big commodious house,
> she felt a return of the tide of last night's irritation, a renewal of
> everything she could secretly suffer from ugliness and stupidity.
> Why did she consent to such contacts, why did she so rashly
> expose herself? She had had, heaven knew, her reasons, but the
> whole experience was to be sharper than she had feared. To get
> away from it and out into the air, into the presence of sky and
> trees, flowers and birds was a necessity of every nerve. (1)

The passage depicts a woman of many things, but the chief one
is anger (and this underlies much of what she feels throughout the
book). Anger is a concentrated and in that respect simple emotion,

not perhaps so complex or far-reaching as the emotion, or rather feeling, expressed by Strether at a certain point near the conclusion of *The Ambassadors* thirteen years after *The Spoils* came out. The hero reflects both the change in himself and the change *that* reflects in his relation to Marie. There is a strong affection, a deep sense of history, but also a sense of something almost uncanny. It is the sense that something is about to happen, we are on the brink of a great change, but that change will be violence:

> Didn't she just wish to assure him that *she* now took it all and so kept it [his ordeal]; that he was absolutely not to worry any more, was only to rest on her laurels and continue generously to help her? The light in her beautiful, formal room was dim, though it would do, as everything would always do . . . . The windows were all open, their redundant hangings swaying a little, and he heard once more, from the empty court, the small plash of the fountain. From beyond this, and as from a great distance—beyond the court, beyond the *corps de logis* forming the front—came, as if excited and exciting, the vague voice of Paris. Strether had all along been subject to sudden gusts of fancy in connection with such matters as these—odd starts of the historic sense, suppositions and divinations with no warrant but their intensity. Thus and so, on the eve of the great recorded dates, the days and nights of revolution, the sounds had come in, the omens, the beginnings broken out. They were the smell of revolution; the smell of the public temper—or perhaps simply the smell of blood. (335; 12, I)

Consciousness has been portrayed as many things by different writers, but the basic component that all have in common is the flow. The flow occurs with rapidity in all states except transcendental consciousness. Primarily, two states of consciousness in James interest us: "ordinary" and "extra-ordinary," or waking and transcendental consciousness. Enormous developments in scientific experiments have provided us with data that will enable us to understand—intellectually—what Henry James "merely" intuited (although William James pointed in the direction of these more recent discoveries). Science distinguishes at least five states of consciousness. The first three are sleeping, dreaming and waking.[4] The

---

[4] Basic research that distinguishes the first three states of consciousness:
(1) Nathaniel Kleitman in *Sleep and Wakefulness*, a starting reference book on sleep in general showing how it differs physiologically from being awake.
(2) *Current Research on Sleep and Dreams* compiled by the Department of

fourth state, transcendental, is commonly reached through medita-tion. The fifth state is sometimes called "all-inclusive" or "enlight-ened" consciousness. Extensive laboratory experiments are already being performed on the fifth state.

In real life, the fifth state involves the sleeping, dreaming, and waking states integrated with transcendental consciousness. Because we do not have to deal with the first two of these in this fictional study, we will speak of the fifth state alone as the second level, the means of integration of waking and transcendental consciousness. Also, the fifth state is in certain systems actually followed by two others, but since the chief function of these is a refinement of the integration of the fifth, I can develop my main thesis without complicating matters by including them. Finally, the states of consciousness are not described merely through subjective experience. They have been explored in several hundred scientific experiments and have been so well identified separately that one can recognize the state a person is in if he is wired for a physiological experiment (as astronauts are wired) simply by reading the monitoring instruments. In the future I will discuss two states: waking or ordinary, and transcendental or extra-ordinary. I will *also* refer to them sometimes as "First and Second Levels."

In complete transcendence, the mind has gone beyond sense experience—to direct perception of pure consciousness or "being"—which means beyond thought or feelings or intuitions or anything in the first three states. Though it is difficult to describe it directly, one can describe pure consciousness indirectly, not only from reports of those who have experienced it repeatedly, but also from strong indicators arising from scientific tests on subjects actually

---

Health Education and Welfare describes research up to 1965 for the nonspe-cialist.

(3) *The Biology of Dreaming* by Earnest Hartmann contains tables listing phys-iological correlates of the wakeful, dreaming, and deep-sleep states.

(4) A 1968 Public Health Service manual contains actual EEG, EOG, and EMG recordings of college students as they go from waking to sleeping to dreaming states.

(5) In an experiment reported in *The International Journal of Neuroscience,* David Orme-Johnson and Christopher T. Haynes examined EEG Phase Co-herence, Pure Consciousness, Creativity, and TM Sidhi experiences. (The TM Sidhi Program is an advanced meditation technique.) Subjects with the most stabilized transcendental consciousness (the simplest form of awareness) were found to have maximum mind-body coordination. Also, the subtlest level of consciousness appears to be a field of all possibilities correlated with maximum creativity.

meditating.[5] During the waking state, the mind is always focused either on an object or an idea of an object. In transcendental consciousness the mind is simply "conscious," with no object to be conscious "of"—other than itself. A simple way of picturing the two conditions, waking state and transcendental consciousness, is to imagine a movie on a screen. The images are colorful and in motion, and one hears many sounds. This is like the waking state. Remove the film, but leave the projector light on; there remains only a white screen which forms a "picture" of transcendental consciousness, also called the fourth state, or "pure" consciousness. In the waking state, the mind has boundaries, dictated by the pictures, while the pictureless screen of transcendental consciousness dictates no boundaries. The mind is unchanging yet unlimited, unbounded, and free, as represented (crudely) by the whiteness of the screen.

Usually people achieve transcendental consciousness through some form of meditation. In meditation systems the "fourth state," the achievement of transcendental consciousness *during* meditation, has been given such names as "satori," "samadhi," "peak experience," or "unified consciousness." Other names and definitions are used depending more on location and custom than upon a real difference in the essential experience. The "motionless" quality has been demonstrated in countless experiments (Wallace). Experiments on breath intake, heart rate, galvanic skin response, and brain wave patterns,

---

[5] The scientists who use subjects performing the Transcendental Meditation Program have been cited more frequently than others in this book because they have produced by far the most extensive body of scientific material on consciousness to date (over 400 experiments). The following are some basic studies of transcendence, including the landmark experiments of R. K. Wallace done at the UCLA Physiology Department, and Thorndyke Memorial Laboratory, Harvard Medical School, in the 1970s. These provided the impetus for an avalanche of later scientific work on consciousness:
(1) Robert Keith Wallace, in an experiment performed at the University of California in 1970, reported that the state produced in Transcendental Meditation may be considered a fourth major state of consciousness ("Physiological Effects" 43).
(2) In an experiment report in The American Journal of Physiology, 1971, Wallace, Herbert Benson, and Archie F. Wilson found that physiological changes occurring during the practice of the Transcendental Meditation technique indicate a unique physiological state characterized by deep relaxation (a "hypometabolic condition"), along with mental alertness.
(3) Jean-Paul Banquet, in an article in an Amsterdam journal in 1973, found that subjects practicing the Transcendental Meditation technique showed distinctive EEG changes, including slow, high-amplitude alpha activity extending to anterior channels; theta activity different from sleep; rhythmic amplitude-modulated beta waves present over the whole scalp; and synchronization of anterior and posterior channels.

all indicate a marked slowing down of the physiology and increased coherence in the nervous system and EEG patterns (Banquet). The typical reduction of metabolism for the average meditator is 16 percent within the first few minutes; the metabolism of some advanced meditators slows down considerably more. Spontaneous breath suspensions as long as 53 seconds have been recorded (Farrow).

From the point of view of those who have experienced it, transcendental consciousness has been described as "a breakthrough into reality of one's own true nature," a deep inner-state wherein one is "witness to all that is pure, genuine, vast, and illuminating about oneself" (William Taylor, quoted by Battista 37). Other descriptions refer to the state as one of calmness, order, omniscience, harmony (with nature or the universe), or "unification," or a "whole and boundless relation with everything"—everywhere (Battista 61–62). According to William James,

> [These] states of insight into depths of truth implumbed by the discursive intellect . . . , illuminating revelations full of significance and importance, all inarticulate though they remain, . . . as a rule carry with them a curious sense of authority for all aftertime . . . susceptible[also] to continuous development in what is felt as inner richness and importance. (*Varieties* 318)

Usually the practiced meditator employs some form of sense experience (i.e., some object or idea or thought or sound) to induce his mind to go toward the point of complete transcendence. However, people who do not practice meditation and may never have heard of it seem clearly to have experienced transcendence for longer or shorter periods of time. Wordsworth, for example, did not meditate systematically, but meditators often point to a passage in "Tintern Abbey" as remarkably reminiscent of the transcendence of their own experience:

> . . . that blessed mood;
> In which the burthen of the mystery
> In which the heavy and the weary weight
> Of all this unintelligible world
> Is lightened: — that serene and blessed mood,
> In which the affections gently lead us on, —
> Until, the breath of this corporeal frame
> And even the motion of our human blood
> Almost suspended, we are laid asleep
> In body, and become a living soul:

> While with an eye made quiet by the power
> Of harmony, and the deep power of joy,
> We see into the life of things.

The examples of such experiences in Eastern and Western literary history are legion. Plotinus gives a brief description of one very important aspect of such an experience:[6]

> All that one sees as a spectacle is still external; one must bring the vision within and see no longer in that mode of separation but as we know ourselves . . . then the soul neither sees, nor distinguishes by seeing, nor imagines that there are two things . . . the perceiver is one with the thing perceived.

The following is a description of an experience by Jacob Boehme which occurred in 1600 when he was twenty-five and working as a shoemaker in Goerlitz:

> Sitting one day in his room, his eyes fell upon a burnished pewter dish, which reflected the sunshine with such marvelous splendour that he fell into an inward ectasy, and it seemed to him as if he could now look into the principles and deepest foundations of things. He believed that it was only a fancy, and in order to banish it from his mind he went out upon the green. But here he remarked that he gazed into the very heart of things, the very herbs and grass, and that actual nature harmonized with what he had inwardly seen. He said nothing of this to anyone, but praised and thanked God in silence.

The following is an anonymous experience:

> It was as though my mind broke bounds and went on expanding until it merged with the universe. Mind and universe became *one within the other*. Time ceased to exist. It was all one thing and in a state of infinity. It was as if, willy nilly, I became directly exposed to an entity within myself and nature at large. I seemed to be 'seeing' with another sight in another world . . . .

Certainly one of the clearest and most finely honed images of transcendental consciousness of more recent times was recorded by Eugene Ionesco in his book *Present Past Past Present*:

> Once, long ago, I was sometimes overcome by a sort of grace, a euphoria. It was as if, first of all, every notion, every reality

---

[6] Unless expressly noted otherwise, the quotations on transcendental experiences in the next few pages are from a collection by J. M. Cohen and J. F. Phipps.

was emptied of its content. After this emptiness, after this dizzy spell, it was as if I found myself suddenly at the center of pure ineffable existence; it was as if things had freed themselves of all arbitrary labels, of a framework that didn't suit them, that limited them; social and logical constraint or the need to define them, to organize them, disappeared. It did not seem to me that I was the victim of a nominalist crisis; on the contrary, I think that I became one with the one essential reality, when, along with an immense, serene joy, I was overcome by what I might call the stupefaction of being, the certainty of being, the certainty that the social order, politics, language, organized thought, systems and systemizations, limitations and delimitations were pure nothingness and that the only true thing was this sensation or this feeling or this assurance that I existed and that this "I exist" was wholly sufficient unto itself, and freed of everything that was outside of it. I knew that nothing could prevent me from being, that nothingness or night or doubt no longer had any power over me.

I say that with words that can only disfigure, that cannot describe the light of this profound, total organic intuition which, surging up as it did from my deepest self, might well have inundated everything, covered everything, both my other self and others. (150–51)

The term "cosmic consciousness" has been said to be the invention of a nineteenth-century physician, R. M. Bucke, who wrote a book with that title. In it he gives the following vivid (*third person*) description of a transcendental experience of his own in which this illuminated consciousness came over him. I have quoted it at some length to retain the full impact of his description:

It was in the early spring, at the beginning of his thirty-sixth year. He and two friends had spent the evening reading Wordsworth, Shelley, Keats, Browning, and especially Whitman. They parted at midnight and he had a long drive in a hansom (it was an English city). His mind, deeply under the influence of the ideas, images and emotions called up by the reading and talk of the evening, was calm and peaceful. He was in a state of quiet, of almost passive enjoyment. All at once, without warning of any kind, he found himself wrapped around as it were by a flame-coloured cloud. For an instant he thought of fire, some sudden conflagration in the great city; the next he knew the light was in himself. Directly afterwards came upon him a sense of exultation, of immense joyousness accompanied or immediately followed by an intellectual illumination quite impossible to describe. Into his brain streamed one momentary lightning-flash of the Brahmic splendour which has ever since lightened his life; upon his heart fell one drop of Brahmic bliss, leaving thenceforward for always an aftertaste of heaven. Among other things . . . he saw and knew that the cosmos is not dead matter but a living Presence, that the soul of man is immortal, that the universe is so built and ordered that without peradventure all things work together for the good of each and all, that the foundation principle of the world is what we call love and that the happiness of everyone in the long run is absolutely certain. He claims he learned more within the few seconds during which the illumination lasted than in previous months or even years of study and that he learned much that no study could ever have taught. (7)

Authors Cohen and Phipps comment that Bucke sees eternity "not in the future but as present reality." And they say, "From the moment of Bucke's envelopment in what he calls fire (which other experiencers think of as light), to that in which he found himself still trotting on through the city in the hansom cab, the temporal span was a few seconds. But twenty-five years later, when he wrote this account, he was still living in the light of this revelation, which had seen him through spells of depression. As far as one knows, there was no preparation by Bucke for this experience."

As a meditator regularly experiences the fourth state, as he "dives" regularly into that ocean of "being," and just as regularly returns to activity, stress in his physiology diminishes; encumbrances to his thinking and acting dissolve; he gains in emotional stability and self-control. In other words, as time goes by, *traces of the fourth state of consciousness begin appearing in the meditator's active life outside of meditations*. Eventually, through longer or shorter periods depending on the nervous system of each meditator, the fourth state becomes permanently established during waking consciousness. At that point, both conditions, third and fourth states, "First Level" or ordinary consciousness and "Second Level"[7] or extra-ordinary

---

[7] (1) In 1975 Dr. Barry Blackwell and several distinguished colleagues did an experiment on the effects of Transcendental Meditation on blood pressure, showing a decrease in blood pressure and anxiety after practicing the TM technique.

(2) In 1975 Andre Tjoa did an experiment showing that the development of nonverbal fluid intelligence was brought about by the practice of Transcendental Meditation.

(3) In 1972 William Seeman and two colleagues found evidence that meditators, over a period of time, developed increased self-actualization.

(4) An experiment by Phil Ferguson and John C. Gowan in 1976 showed

consciousness, function simultaneously: when this happens—when the two states appear on the same level permanently—the person is on the brink of being "enlightened."[8] "Enlightened" is a term used loosely in Western vocabularies, but in Eastern systems it refers to a specific state of development in which the process of evolutionary growth has continued, causing the two stages to integrate more and more until total unified consciousness has been reached. An enlightened person lives permanently in this condition.

In meditation itself, before any of the above experiences take place, one notices one's mind changing from a state of "surface" activity to complete silence. Gradually the mind settles down until it transcends[9] surface activity altogether and then it experiences that "pure" or "nonvibrating" consciousness, the fourth state, mentioned earlier in this chapter with the other states of consciousness. Thus in meditation the mind does literally progress from that motion to the motionlessness I have mentioned in connection with Lambert Strether.

From the time he enters Gloriani's garden until he finally prepares to leave for Woollett, Strether is continually undergoing activities that bring his mind to that motionlessness which can be identified with transcendental consciousness. The experience of transcendence, of order, calm, insight, spontaneity, and harmony with nature, is always initiated in and by his visits with Marie de Vionnet. After these visits he returns to the realm of activity; he meets Chad; he meets Miss Barrace; he meets Little Bilham, and others. As a person meditates more and more, as he emerges more and more from the transcendent experience, so he will understand

reduced negativity traits and an increasing self-actualization that was marked and cumulative as a result of consistent practice of Transcendental Meditation. (5) Another 1973 experiment by David Orme-Johnson demonstrated that meditating subjects show greater autonomic stability ("Autonomic").
(6) In 1974 David Frew found improvement in job performance, job satisfaction, job stability, and interpersonal relationships with co-workers and supervisors among people practicing the Transcendental Meditation technique.

[8] Maharisha-Mahesh Yogi, the founder of Transcendental Meditation, says: "The ability of man's nervous system, which is the physical machinery through which consciousness expresses itself, has to be developed to express these two states or levels simultaneously. This is brought about by regularly interrupting the constant activity of the waking state of consciousness with periods of silence in transcendental consciousness. When, through this practice, the nervous system has been permanently conditioned to maintain these two states together, then the consciousness remains centered in the Self [meaning the Universal Self, meaning fulfilled or 'enlightened']" (Bhagavad-Gita 226).

[9] The term "transcend" is used to mean "go beyond" as opposed to "rise above."

more and more ordinary, active experience from the perspective of the transcendent experience. At the end of six such sessions with the Countess, Strether undergoes the final moment of transcendence I referred to in the opening lines of this chapter. Immediately after that, he explains that *now* it will be necessary to integrate the Woollett experience with the Paris one, just as the meditator eventually integrates the First and Second Levels on a permanent basis.

During these scenes, Marie acts as teacher, intermediary, or "daimon," in Shelley's sense of the term, and the result of her effort is to lead Strether away from surface restlessness, unsureness, anxiety, complexity, and confusion. At the same time, she leads him *toward* rest, conviction, calm, trust, resolution, simplicity, and order—just as the meditation process, when properly carried out, allows the mind to be drawn by its own natural inclinations from surface activity to the total silence of pure consciousness.

Some, if not most, who describe transcendence speak of it as a gradual settling down, as if the mind were physically undergoing a "downward" progression. Henry James describes Strether's experiences as if his mind were undergoing just such a movement; he says Strether "dives" from his previous condition: "For an hour, in the matter of letting himself go, of diving deep [he] was to feel that he had touched bottom" (184; 7: I). Again, he often talks of his situation, his journey of the mind, as if he is being taken over by something beyond him: "The sense he had had before, the sense he had had repeatedly, the sense that the situation was running away from him, had never been so sharp as now" (184). At another point he surrenders to her as if crossing over to her side: "If all the accidents were to fight on her side—and by actual showing they loomed large—he could only give himself up" (185). If he *should* at last cross that line, what would happen? He would undoubtedly "see things her way." But if we assume that he does later achieve this transcendent state during his everyday activities, then he is destined to see things in the manner of others before him who have reached that level; as Plotinus, for example who says, "The perceiver is one with the thing perceived" (Cohen and Phipps 13). He will then perceive some fundamental aspect of her consciousness that is the same as his: glimpses simultaneously of his transcendent self in her and in himself.

This is what does happen, as we begin to find in their next visit. The first time Strether visits Marie alone after Gloriani's garden party he foreshadows, in the "picture" sequence which so often precedes an important scene in James, the ultimate sense of the scene itself—and what he will be "taught" by Marie. He will, he gathers from a first view of the house, be given peace, the "peace of intervals, the dignity of distances and approaches . . . " (151; 6, I); he will be given "the Paris that he was always looking for"; he will be given something "hereditary, cherished, charming." He will be given the "glory" of an ideal—in the form of his (and James's) beloved First Empire. The mistress of the scene before him (in the matter of acquiring objects for her salon) had only "received, accepted, and been quiet" (152). He had been given "the consciousness of private honour," "the air of respectability" that found "the clearest medium of its particular kind that he had ever breathed." He finds her, personally, completely "new" to him (as is his experience of transcendence), with "a rare unlikeness to women he had known." And he finds her motionless, seated "with . . . hands clasped in her lap and no movement, in all of her person, but the fine prompt play of her deep young face" (153). In transcendental consciousness nature acts, yet remains motionless; one experiences silence, yet activity. It is "restful alertness."

Strether catches sight of qualities in this picture similar to those found in the Gloriani passage: peacefulness, order, charm, silence, acceptance, newness, and finally motionlessness, as if one were capable, he says, of "letting things be" as he puts it some time later (179; 7, I). The following excerpts from the scene in question show Marie deliberately, but gently, leading him away from his old mind:

M: Well . . . the only thing that really matters is that you shall get on with me.
S: (betraying again his "surface restlessness"): Ah, but I don't!
M: Will you consent to go on with me a little—provisionally—as if you did? (Upon which she raises "from somewhere below him her suppliant beautiful eyes.")

In the next exchange she protests that she is not simply following Chad's orders by trying to win him over:

M: This is my own idea and a different thing.
S: I was sure a moment since that some idea of your own had come to you.
M: I made out you were sure—and that helped it to come. So you see, we do get on.

Thus negative Strether has turned positive; an unwilling Strether has become not unwilling. A moment later, Strether comments to himself, "He couldn't help it; it wasn't his fault; he had done nothing, but by a turn of the hand she had somehow made their encounter a relation" (154).

By the end of the scene, he has discovered the extent of that "relation":

> At the back of his head, behind everything, was a sense that she was—there, before him, close to him, in vivid imperative form,— one of the rare women he had so often heard of, read of, but never met, whose very presence, look, voice, the mere contemporaneous *fact* of whom, from the moment it was all presented, made a relation of mere recognition. That was not the kind of woman he had ever found Mrs. Newsome, a contemporaneous fact who had been distinctly slow to establish herself. (156)

A relation of mere recognition. In order to have a reciprocating relation of any meaning with Marie, he must have it in terms of what she "is"—that is, "is" most essentially. What she "is" in terms of being is what Strether has discovered, by his intuition, in the picture scene: orderly, silent, etc. In other words, he senses the deeper consciousness—transcendental or "pure"—that influences her actions and may indeed be the foundation of them; but he is able to recognize such a quality only insofar as he possesses it himself. He cannot sustain the fullness of it at all times because it is a discovery, really, about his own self that is new to him. However, when he makes contact with someone who is rooted in it, a bridge appears, "an added link and certainly a common priceless ground for them to meet upon" (337; 12, I), and he later describes his own relation with her and Chad. Thus, as Marie "functions" on the Second Level, Strether begins to find himself capable of doing the same. The *communication* the two have is shifting to the transcendental level and involves more openness and recognition than at any time before.

As I have said, the "method" Strether undergoes consists of alternating transcendence and everyday activity. The alternation at first takes him back and forth from Marie de Vionnet's presence (and transcendent influence) to everyday Paris. Of course, each cycle should find him in a more "transcendent" condition. A complex problem might take many such cycles before it could be resolved, that is, before the "light" permeated every aspect of his mind to the point where it would be absorbed in the clarity and settled orderliness of the *other*, the Second, level of consciousness.

Two serious problems face Strether as he departs from his friend's salon at this moment in the story; the first involves his identity. As he grows, the transcendence he has "gathered" at Marie's will begin to function without his always returning to see her. The first time this happens he gets a tremendous assist in his understanding from the metaphorical "source" of the light; in Chad's flat, he re-encounters Gloriani. Gloriani is busy studying a French landscape, and his approval of it marks a settlement of "many things once for all" (162; 6, II), as Strether says. For one thing, it is an acceptance by Gloriani of the quality of Chad's art collection. Gloriani, who could be called arbiter of taste for all of Paris, is at the center of the life that was presumed to be ruining Chad. Now Strether learns that Chad not only has gained exquisite taste but also has had it unconditionally approved by the Master. As Gloriani glances at Strether, he compares himself to him. Gloriani, like the man with the scar in "The Beast in the Jungle," is a person steeped in experience, while Strether is a mere noninvolved observer—or considers himself so at this point in his growth. Gloriani works in clay (he is man) and molds experience (he is creation). Strether is learning to see things with a universal vision; Gloriani already reveals such a vision on his part by what he has accomplished with his hands. True, Strether's reaction *earlier* might have been a sense of inferiority alongside this giant of a man, as John Marcher probably felt watching the stranger at May's tomb in "The Beast in the Jungle." But now, bolstered by his light, Strether sees the contrast as *sharpening* his own identity. "Strether was conscious, at this instant, . . . as he hadn't been, of how round about him, quite without him [things] *were* consistently settled." Though Gloriani's smile was indefinite, the "momentary link [had been] supplied . . . doubt between them had snapped. [Strether] was conscious now of the final reality, which was that there wasn't so much a doubt as a difference altogether" (163; 6, II). He has Gloriani's wave-length now; there is no doubt, he realizes, that the transcendent level of consciousness, and the vision it involves, is something they have in common, but their ways of achieving it differ: Strether's means is sight; Gloriani's is touch.

As Gloriani's occupaton is weighted on the side of doing, Strether's is weighted on the side of seeing. Seeing is no more a completely static process than consciousness; if one is to transcend one's past, one's seeing ability must grow. Strether is openly aware of this way of seeing. He speaks of "the growing rose of observation, constantly stronger for him, he felt, in scent and color, and in which he could bury his nose even to wantonness" (163). As Strether develops, seeing then will move toward "being." But also seeing as "being"—and seeing *and doing*—will all occur together if and when he reaches full integration.

Strether has resolved the first of his two major problems (the problem of identity), enough at least to enable him to go on with greater ease (163). The second major problem is the one he has about the "virtuous [or nonvirtuous] attachment" of Chad and Marie, which is the subject of the next chapter.

"VIRTUOUS ATTACHMENTS"

As the growth in Strether continues, as the alternating of the activity and the "silence" originating in the salon of Mme. de Vionnet and carried by him into the outer world goes on, Strether experiences further changes in his consciousness. One of these changes involves his understanding of the affair of Chad and Marie. In the beginning, he had the impression that this affair was a "virtuous" one meaning, to Strether, platonic. This notion satisfied his deepest puritanical soul. Near the story's end, he discovers that he has been misinformed: the affair is sexual and has been so all along. His reaction then is anything but puritanical. From his first impression to his last, he has undergone many smaller changes in attitude and, in a sense, the growth he makes throughout the novel can be measured by his changing attitudes toward the affair of Chad and Marie.

The question of the virtue of the attachment is first broached in an early scene with Gostrey (45; 2, I) in which the two of them speculate about a hypothetical wicked woman (G.: "Are you quite sure she's bad for him?" S.: "Wouldn't you be?"). Afterwards he meets and is overwhelmed by the charm of the real woman in question. From the time Bilham makes his notorious remark that the affair is virtuous ("Little Bilham looked him full in the face: 'Because it's a virtuous attachment,'") (116; 4, II) until the truth is exposed to Strether in the river scene, the novel does not supply an explicit account of Strether's attitudes and feelings about the matter. Yet we know that by the time he sees Marie at the end, a revolution has occurred. And in the end, when he discovers the kind of relationship the couple has had, he reverses his position and ends up supporting it. Something, or several things, then, occurred in the meantime to bring about this reversal.

The revolution centers on two subjects, Strether's developing consciousness and his altered attitude toward sexual intimacy. To understand what is responsible for the change in Strether and what the change involves, it is helpful to explore several related factors— first, James's life, in that his discovery of sex and sexual intimacy (so far as he did discover the latter) provides a background to events in this and other of his novels; second, Strether's change in psychological and sexual understanding insofar as it reflects the changing historical attitude toward sexual knowledge before, during and after the lifetime of Henry James; and third, the change in Strether's level of consciousness, since that affects not merely Strether's attitude toward sex, but his attitude about life.

To examine these factors I will turn away from the direct discussion of The Ambassadors temporarily and give a glimpse of Henry James's personal experience. I will then take a long look at The Portrait of a Lady, partly because that work gives many clues to the nature of this change and also substantiates my contention that a particular combination of spiritual-sexual change is common to many of James's major writings. But mainly The Portrait contains evidence that, as his career progressed, he made a conscious effort to dramatize the spiritual aspect of the change with increasing frequency through the transcendence of his major characters. Henry James revised The Portrait of a Lady within a few years of completing The Ambassadors. The Ambassadors was published in 1902; The Portrait first appeared in 1881 but was thoroughly revised between 1906 and 1907. The revision of The Portrait indicates a development in terms of spiritual-sexual understanding which involves the position of Henry James at the time of completing or just after the time of publishing The Ambassadors in 1902.

Finally, in order to clarify the nature of the sexual-spiritual change, I will summarize the principles St. Augustine set down on the sexual-spiritual "dilemma" of man in general and apply those principles to The Portrait and to The Ambassadors.

Was there anything in James's own life that could have predisposed him to write about a liberating change in his characters' attitudes about sex? It was not until his later novels that he began to allow, however guardedly, physical sex to become a reality in his work. The ability to show natural affection and openness of feeling apparently came to him only late in life. Leon Edel describes how James's upbringing kept him (intentionally or not) from finding out about sex as a boy and even as a young man, and how he "ended up with a personal aloofness which probably shut him into auto-eroticism. He lived his private sexual life as if he were an anchorite . . . " (James, *Letters* xv). In the middle years, he went through a period in his work of intense curiosity about matters sexual. And in 1899 he finally experienced "sensations of love, the body's insistence on active tenderness" when he met and became unusually affectionate with Hendrik Anderson. Edel explains, "The drama of their encounter was that of an aging novelist who was living out certain submerged adolescent feelings and divesting himself of puritanical wrappings."[1] James's experience with the young sculptor was not an isolated phenomenon; other events in his life at that time aided in his shuffling off the puritanical coils:

> When James was writing *The Sacred Fount*, he became friends with Stephen Crane and his mistress, Cora. Cora had once kept a brothel called the 'Hotel de Dream' in Florida. Ten years earlier James might have held back stiffly from her and her open ways. But now he is neighborly; he goes to their parties, munches Cora's doughnuts, and contributes money to help the illegitimate children of the American novelist, Harold Frederick, recently dead of a coronary. This takes place in the context of the last of James's novels of bewilderment. He can now write *The Ambassadors*, with its theme of 'live all you can' . . . . Once his armor is breached, James can handle the sensuous and the physical but he still wears the soft gloves of the genteel tradition . . . (James, *Letters* xviii).

Such a pattern of sexual discovery involving a growing flexibility of attitude and understanding undoubtedly fostered the maturing attitude found in a number of James's works, but especially in *The Ambassadors* and the revised *Portrait of a Lady*. In James, often a hero of uncommon innocence gets into a marriage and later real-

---

[1] Edel adds that James probably never "acted out the physical promptings of sex, but, prior to the composition of *The Ambassadors* he did become more affectionate socially, kissing friends, hugging them, and patting them on the back" (James, *Letters* xix).

izes the deception of a partner, a deception that almost always has a connection with sex. The character first registers shock, then makes another larger discovery about his short-sightedness, which in turn leads to a choice based on a different order of consciousness than he has experienced at any time before. In the case of *The Ambassadors*, Strether's new consciousness leads to a renewed and different appreciation of the intimacy (both sexual and otherwise) of his two friends, and as a result he even attempts to get them to go on with their "nonvirtuous" attachment.

The Ambassadors is probably the best model in the James canon to use in illustrating the complete cycle of this sexual-spiritual drama, partly because both elements of the change are manifested in one novel (as they are not totally, for example, in *The Portrait*), but equally important, the *transcendences* in *The Ambassadors* are utterly clear. At the same time the revised edition of *The Portrait of a Lady* clarifies the development in Henry James that enabled him to do what he did in *The Ambassadors*. In the first version of *The Portrait* both elements, sexual and spiritual, are evident in the plot but neither is quite so precisely and elegantly detailed as in the second. A careful comparison shows that the revised version of *The Portrait*—if one regards *The Ambassadors* momentarily as an interim preparation for that novel—makes the experience of the heroine at the end of *The Portrait* more recognizably transcendent. It is through transcendence that she discovers a way out of her sexual dilemma and simultaneously glides into a sea of wider understanding.

The heroine of *The Portrait*, Isabel Archer, after unexpectedly inheriting a fortune, rejects two superbly eligible suitors and, against the advice of her good friend and cousin, Ralph Touchett, marries Gilbert Osmond, who, though not wealthy, prides himself on his impeccable taste, manners, and decorum. Gilbert's daughter, Pansy, and an old friend and confidante, Mme. Merle, are much closer friends than Isabel had recognized. The insight gives her serious pause and, in the long scene of her musing before the fire, she realizes that her husband not only does not love her but simply despises her. He seems to have married her to have someone to look down upon, not aware of the extent of his own envy, which later turned into recognizable hatred (1881, Chapter 42). As this side of his character emerges out of Isabel's musings, Gilbert reveals himself as the subtle manipulator of her freedom of choice, of her right to live as a person. The effect of his misuse leaves her confused, despairing, and spiritually dying; then she arrives at another realization (a realization more about herself than the couple involved), when, in the drawing room at Rome she makes the discovery about Mme. Merle and Gilbert. It is a discovery that eventually leads to a vastly clearer understanding of Osmond, of Ralph, and of herself; and in the final love scene with Caspar Goodwood she undergoes a tremendous reinforcement of the insight gained in that first scene. (It is during this last experience that she makes up her mind to reject Caspar and return to Gilbert). The choice is made through a realization that corresponds to Lambert Strether's in many ways because, when she finally decides, she has encompassed a different dimension of awareness and incorporated a different understanding of the people closest to her. Together these last two conceptions form themselves into a touchstone deep in her mind on which to test her future moves.

Some elucidation of Isabel's situation is provided by the second chapter of the Book of Genesis, as Dorothy Van Ghent has indicated in identifying life with the two trees, the Tree of the Fall and the Tree of the Resurrection. According to her, Isabel Archer, in a voluntary search for "connoisseurs," under an illusion of perfect freedom, chose an evil—chose what she thought to be the "best" in experience. Later, through suffering, she says, insight came and the "fructification" of consciousness (211–14). Lyall Powers, advancing this thesis, shows how Gardencourt is like an Eden, a "sacred place"; how the first nine chapters of the novel are devoted in great part to establishing Isabel's "prelapsarian innocence"; how Gilbert Osmond is "the serpent in the bank of flowers"; and how Ralph stands opposed to him as a Christ-like figure. She chooses to marry Gilbert, the "devil"-figure and the choice precipitates her fortunate "fall."

Thus the early myth couples with the Christian drama as an overriding structural metaphor. Isabel's problem is the same as Adam's. Her self-sufficiency and independence were laudable traits in one sense, but when they became self-defined, they became misguided, and as such they became self-willed. Self-will and a higher awareness or higher power became the larger elements of her conflict.

Isabel's life can be seen to follow loosely three phases: an innocence, a fall, and a redemption. The first is a sexual innocence as well as an innocence about life in general prior to her marriage; her "fall" can be considered her mistaken marital choice; her redemption or self-realization begins with the drawing room scene in Chapter 40 and continues through several further discoveries until the final explosive scene with Caspar.

It is difficult to label Isabel's "fault," as if she really had a main fault. She is Everywoman; her fault is innocence, and therefore ignorance, of experience. It is destined that Everywoman will make mistakes. Isabel's situation, in the innocence phase, like Adam's, is ambivalent: she has a desire to be free and independent—a noble aim; that tendency can easily become arrogance. She has a "normal" caution, or fear, about life and all its dangers, including sexual relations; but she also has a lack of the experience and knowledge combined that could make it easier for her to choose the right person to marry.[2]

One undercurrent seems to run through all Isabel's characteristics: she has an inability to surrender fully to any deep experience; accompanying this trait and probably related to it is her tendency to want to control experience. She was looking for a husband, but she was at the same time always in the act of determining for herself when and if to fall in love. First she must determine whether the suitor fits her image of "the best"—and she must do so by the experimental European tour. She planned to fall in love after she had made an appraisal of life on her own terms. The next logical step after controlling experience is to try to possess it. She took that step when she decided to marry Gilbert and make him her "property" (Norton ed. 358; 42).

Perhaps the underlying reason Isabel "fell into" a wrong choice was that her experience so far in this early phase of her life gave her no certain knowledge of its meaning; that is, her choice might have been different had she had more knowledge about erotic love, but more important than that, knowledge about the relationship of erotic love to spiritual love. Isabel may have feared a loss of freedom generally if she accepted Warburton or Goodwood; she may also have feared "erotic involvement" of the kind that would lead to forfeiting freedom to such suitors. Such was not the case with Gilbert; the erotic element of Mrs. Osmond's life—"so admirably

---

[2] Anthony Mazzella comments in the Norton Edition of The Portrait: "It is a fear that her freedom will be lost through erotic possession" (609). In developing this, Mazzella sees the white lightning in the final scene as a fear; to me it is an internal signal of transcendental consciousness (for elaboration see this chapter, p. 78, and the Appendix, p. 148). If Isabel had a fear of sex and its accompanying repercussions early on and the same fear at the very end, the implication would be that the profound intervening experiences of her life have produced no significant change, and especially no significant improvement, which would be absurd.

intimate at first"—was not frightening, possibly because she thought that instead of being possessed by him she had made him her "property."

By contrast to Isabel, Gilbert was objective, urbane, intelligently cerebral, yet agreeable (at first), and had one more trait most significant to Isabel: splendid taste in everything. Furthermore, his attitude in the beginning gave Isabel confidence that she would not be overwhelmed by an erotic storm. In fact, sexually he appeared to be gentle, even reticent: "He was like a sceptical voyager strolling on the beach while he waited for the tide, looking seaward yet not putting to sea" (357). And he at least spoke as if the two of them would be equal and free:

> Hadn't he all the appearance of a man living in the open air of the world, indifferent to small considerations caring only for truth and knowledge and believing that two intelligent people ought to look for them together, and whether they found them or not, find at least some happiness in the search? (359)

Through Gilbert, Isabel chose "safety" to protect her freedom and individuality, and in her innocence, inexperience, and naive overcertainty she got perhaps the most suffocating—not necessarily erotically suffocating though she says at one point they "don't live decently together" (447; 50)—partner Europe could produce. At first, when she married Gilbert, Isabel gained the "experience" of love; at first, she said he had been "originally at least, so tender." In a few months, as his hostility grew, the intimacy stopped, the agreeability disappeared. He told her he "detested" women with ideas, and then: "The things she . . . said were answered only by his scorn, and she could see he was ineffably ashamed of her" (362).

The "redemptive" phase, starting in the drawing room scene where she gets the insight into Osmond and Mme. Merle, reflects a refreshing, creative awakening in Isabel's mind. The phase culminates in the final scene with Caspar when she surrenders to an utterly radiant spiritual experience (immediately following the sexual one). This last experience enables her to see with a clearer vision the relation of sexual experience and all the rest of experience to transcendental consciousness.

These phases of her life, as abbreviated as they appear here, indicate that a sexual problem—not an extreme one, not an abnormal one—was there and was something she must cope with; and indeed the sexual problem related to the other elements of her conflict, self-will and higher awareness. St. Augustine helps clarify the relationship between self-will, higher awareness and the sexual problem. Augustine treats their configuration as a general problem of humanity, and speaks in moral and philosophical language; Henry James treats the problem in a dramatic and personal way. James leaves us with the problem. St. Augustine leaves us with a solution which helps us understand James.

Before Isabel experienced her awakening to higher consciousness, she still perceived the world from a state of "ordinary" consciousness (as defined in my Chapter III). She saw Lord Warburton, Caspar Goodwood, Gilbert Osmond, and even Ralph Touchett from the perspective of the First Level, the ordinary, or in a terminology more compatible with St. Augustine's, she saw with a "worldly" vision. She later discovers within herself an unworldly vision or an "extra-ordinary" consciousness—the Second Level. She recognizes that Ralph is (as is Mme. de Vionnet to Strether) the one person for her to turn to when she has had enough of worldliness. In fact, the author has signalled this quality in Ralph to the reader: Ralph is singularly unsuited to this world; he is also mortally ill and about to leave this world.

In Chapter 14 of *The City of God*, St. Augustine identifies forms or levels of love (449). He alludes to the Pauline distinction between living "after the flesh" and living "after the spirit." His argument focuses on the emphasis St. Paul and subsequent generations placed upon the two concepts. Augustine shows that the dilemma is not merely a question of spirit *contra* flesh (or matter). When one loves after the spirit, he has the "right will," that is, "well-directed love." The "wrong will" is "ill-directed love" (460). He explains the mistaken attachment of ill-directed love to "the flesh" and well-directed love to "the spirit." Sin, he explains, readily becomes lust, lust being at that time the generic word for all desires; thus sin is usually associated with sexual passion. "Much human sin," he says, "takes effect through the *dependence* of human generation on sexual passion." Augustine was subsequently attacked by the Pelagian Bishop Julian for linking "original sin with sexuality." If the ensuing debate did not originate, it certainly heightened the confusion of sex with sin that has lasted through centuries. Augustine, in Chapter 14, is careful to point out that there is "no necessary division between *amor* and *caritas*" (449)—erotic and charitable love. Living after the flesh was not purely and simply indulging in carnal pleasure; it could take the *form* of carnal pleasure, and very often tended to do so. On the other hand, one might indulge in sexual pleasure and *not* be involved in ill-directed love. To Augustine the term "ill-directed love" meant loving the world instead of the Father (to reiterate, this relation to the "world" is *roughly* equivalent to the First Level of consciousness as I have defined it with reference to *The Ambassadors*); "Good" consisted in living after the Father in "well-directed love." Sin, then, consisted in making the wrong choice with respect to the will of the Father. In sin, first comes the act of man's will, after which one's love might grow lustful in the sexual sense or in *any other sense* depending on the situation. (Bishop Julian had accused him of saying the opposite of what he really had meant.)

Augustine is also careful to explain that the well-directed love of Adam and Eve before the fall *necessarily included consummation of the sexual act:*

> The blessing upon marriage which encouraged them to increase and multiply . . . after they had sinned, was yet given before they had sinned . . . But now [after the fall] men being ignorant of the blessedness of Paradise, suppose that children could not have been begotten there in any other way than they knew them to be begotten now, i.e., by lust, at which [now] even honorable marriage blushes. (469)

The couple did have sexual relations before the Fall, but without "lust." Since then mankind has conveniently over-simplified the meaning of the whole problem by saying: since sex itself is lustful, it is therefore evil; *therefore,* before the Fall, Adam and Eve (since obviously they were virtuous) must not have had sex. To Augustine, the sexual act and sexual pleasures were "good" (i.e., well-directed) before the Fall, and *could* be so afterwards. The later misconception deriving from what he had said caused many to think: "Good 'equals' asceticism; evil 'equals' carnal love."[3]

---

[3] The misconception grew and went on for centuries. In the figures on the Bernward Doors for the Hildesheim Cathedral (ca. 1015) the scenes showing the Fall of Man depicted Adam and Eve as sexless and almost indistinguishable. But following the expulsion from the Garden, Eve suddenly becomes female, has a bare breast, and nurses a child. After the Papal edict of 1097 requiring celibacy of all clergy, the church's position, reflected in many forms of art, showed an increasingly closer association of sex with evil. Demons, until that time rather small, benign creatures, became distorted, enlarged, more diabolical and sexually sadistic. Conversely, as the pattern was reflected in certain forms of art, spiritual good became associated with sexual continence. By the time of Hieronymous Bosch, for example, in "The Temptation of St. Anthony"

I do not insist that Isabel, in order to achieve the measure of "well-directed love" she did, had to achieve it in the form of conscious intellectual understanding, because the knowledge was about herself with respect to her own relationships and could have been felt or sensed but not articulated. On the other hand, Lambert Strether, whose very success in his mission depended on having a conscious understanding (because he had to make an objective judgment about his two friends) probably, after his transcendent experiences, did learn and could articulate where and how everything fitted so far as his own mental attitude was concerned. And, not in the same form, but in some form, most of the problems here are problems Strether also had to come to terms with before he could make a decision about his friends' affair.

Throughout the novel, Isabel's consciousness shows an ascent from ordinary (or "ignorant") consciousness to extra-ordinary or "higher" consciousness, from "ill-directed" to "well- directed" love, and in addition, a sense of the relationship of sex to these concepts *later* that goes far beyond the ordinary.

But what is St. Augustine's lesson about sex and higher consciousness, and does it help answer our questions about Isabel? The lesson is that higher consciousness—or extraordinary consciousness, the "Will of the Father" (to satisfy St. Augustine) should be involved with all of consciousness, including ordinary consciousness, of which sex is a part. If the "Will" of Augustine's passage were the "light," the light should invade every corner of consciousness, while no aspect of consciousness, be it erotic love or possessiveness or any activity, should eclipse the light. From the first part of the story up to the time of her marriage and afterwards, one could say Isabel lived by "ill-directed love." One could characterize her problem before the Fall, as I began to earlier, by saying she was unable to surrender to anything or anybody. Her "proper" puritanical attitude is seen in her response to Ralph's saying, early on, she wants to "drain the cup of experience": she says she doesn't want to *touch* the cup—"it's a poisoned drink" (Norton ed. 134).

By the time of her marriage to Gilbert Osmond, had Isabel ever been in Love? After being courted by three men—all of whom had admirable though not perfect qualifications—one might expect, but for the fact that she carried in her imagination an unrealizable ideal,

(ca. 1510), the entire motif of the temptation consisted of a saint being tempted away from celibacy by demons.

she might succumb to at least one of them. The fact is, until near the end of the novel, falling in love had been a matter of her own, self-directed "edification."

Behind her inability to surrender to love was the illusion that the adventure and experience she was meant to gain should be reached out for and taken into her. She was looking for her fate as if it were something to be acquired. As it turned out, it was. It became a heavy burden.

Her tragic fate, after her choice, was that she placed her gifts and ability in the hands of someone like Gilbert. And when they married, Gilbert certainly did become guilty of misusing Isabel cruelly—but this is not the essential problem of the heroine's life. Once either of them had decided to "reach for" and "possess," they *both* lived in a state of mutual hostility and despair—despair of the kind that Ralph noticed with astonishment and Isabel vividly saw in Chapter 42. Once married, they were both continually shocked that the other partner did not live up to their preconceived notions of Paradise. Not that Gilbert believed in Paradise, but he did make it plain that he would take to himself "a young lady who had qualified herself to figure in his collection of choice objects."

For Isabel, after she recognized her mistake, the problem of whether to return to Osmond was neither a matter of practicality or even of prudence. Her conflict was not vis-à-vis Gilbert, not shaping his fate or hers in connection with him *primarily*: it was a battle with her own fate. Many would say that her disentanglement from her problems, sexual and spiritual, resulted from Isabel's recognizing what was evil in Gilbert and even in herself, and, at some point, what was "good" in Ralph. I agree with this interpretation as a beginning. In his last visit with Isabel just before his death, Ralph, as always, offers—and shares—his love, which as far as she knew until that day had only been a loving friendship; at the end of the visit he tells her he "adores" her. Earlier he had given her a fortune, loved her, and was *in* love with her and now he had openly declared his love; all of this was bound to inspire, stir, and excite her. But why is there such a long period before she realizes and begins to act on the basis of the knowledge he is supposed to have been imparting?

The answer is that none of the knowledge could take effect until her mind underwent a shift in the way it functioned; the shift in turn could make recognition possible.

How did Isabel know what she came to know?

In his Introduction to *The Portrait of a Lady* (Dell ed.), R. P. Blackmur tries to describe the crux of this change or shift in Isabel. (Blackmur, incidentally, says that the shift takes place but does not know precisely what it is that happens.) Referring to the last scene, he says "Isabel flees the passion she has begun to feel . . . she must flee either in acceptance or renunciation—or some peculiar state where the one doubles for the other: a shifting state, somehow not an evasion, in which the sensibilities of James (sic) heroes and heroines so transpire" (6).[4]

These changes (Blackmur calls them *eclaircissements*) in *The Portrait* have their beginnings in the two scenes mentioned above. The first is in the drawing room at Osmond's in Rome (Norton ed. 342; 40). That scene opens the window of her mind to the later famous "recognition" (Chapter 42). The scene is the one in which Isabel sees that more intimacy than she had imagined went on between Mme. Merle and Gilbert. Blackmur says it was of "the knowledge one did not know that one knew, or only dimly knew, that bursts upon one, an access of strength; and it bursts from inside where it has been nurtured with every unconscious skill" (10). Blackmur seems to be describing transcendence or something close to it without being able to identify it precisely. What he is noticing *could* be complete transcendence; that is, in meditative transcending one reaches a point where he can no longer describe what is happening—first a settling of the mind toward increasing stillness and increasingly fine, or subtle, consciousness; after the mind reaches the finest possible consciousness, it transcends, or goes beyond ordinary, everyday consciousness to another level of consciousness. At times the experience just prior to transcending can be seen by the mind's eye; then, in transcendence itself occurs what is sometimes described by individual meditators as darkness, blankness—or "no thoughts." Not enough detailed evidence is given in this passage of *The Portrait* to be certain that Isabel took that last step, but in her performance afterwards and until the end of the story, she continues to burst with new insights, knowledge, and actions; by these we can infer *in hindsight* that she must have transcended. Transcendence is a mind-shift that reverberates in activity outside of the transcendent moment; her insights, knowledge and changed activity appeared immediately

---

[4] Also see the definition of renunciation, that is, my amended definition according to the *Bhagavad-Gita*, in the final pages of Chapter V of this book.

after the scene and persisted until the very end of the book, whereas she had been passive and more or less paralyzed before that event. In the scene where this occurs, Isabel comes in from a walk on the Campagna with Pansy:

> Just beyond the threshold of the drawing-room she stopped short, the reason for her doing so being that she had received an impression. The impression had, in strictness, nothing unprecedented; but she felt it as something new, and the soundlessness of her step gave her time to take in the scene before she interrupted it . . . for a minute they were unaware she had come in. Isabel had often seen that before, certainly; but what she had not seen, or at least had not noticed, was that their colloquy had for the moment converted itself into a sort of familiar silence, from which she instantly perceived that her entrance would startle them . . . . What struck Isabel first was that he was sitting while Mme. Merle stood; there was an anomaly in this that arrested her . . . [they] were musing face to face, with the freedom of old friends who sometimes exchange ideas without uttering them. There was nothing to shock in this; they were old friends, in fact. But the thing made an image, lasting only a moment, like a sudden flicker of light (Norton ed. 342–43).

I quoted all of this because the dramatic tone of the passage is as important a clue to something strange that is happening as are the points made. After this scene, in which she sees their intimacy, she finds out that Mme. Merle arranged her (Isabel's) marriage, Pansy was Mme. Merle's daughter via Gilbert, and the whole plan was to get Isabel's money. But before she learned these things, something "new" had happened, something hitherto unnoticed; the dialogue "converted itself"; what she saw "arrested" her; a sudden "flicker of light" appeared. Chiefly what she is noticing here is the change itself. She is becoming aware that it affects her perception; and apparently (thus far in her discovery) the new perceptions are sharper, and better, in the sense that she is seeing things she had not noticed before.

The new perception represents the beginning of a new form of consciousness; a "form of consciousness" is not something one can reach out for and put in place. Again, it cannot be obtained by "believing" in it. Basically, it is not even a form of thinking. It can perhaps be achieved if the mind can surrender, or open itself, as if a vessel were stored there (some place not noticeable) and if the top were removed the fluid would pour out and saturate the whole organism. Once saturated, the mind would then function from that saturated condition, spontaneously, not deliberately.

The mind finds that condition concealed in its own resources, not the resources of a model, such as another person, though a model might have been critical in introducing the person to his or her new perception. Ralph, for example, could model this condition for Isabel. Her first glimpse of this new ability—this new kind of knowledge—this new light—was evidenced in concrete form a few moments after the drawing room scene above when the recognition of Gilbert's evil flowed out of Isabel in great detail. But the change in the nature of what she saw came from within, from her own deeper consciousness. I repeat: to change levels of consciousness one needs a shift in the basic structure of the mind. And for Isabel, when the evil was once known, the decision of what to do about it might have been "modeled" by Ralph—suggestions might have come from Ralph or others—but the ultimate choice (or surrender) involved in this kind of shift would have to come from her own consciousness. Ralph could even, as it were, hold her up like a child first learning to walk. But that is not how she made her discovery. Her attention was drawn to a particular scene; she took a step; in one second she found her own mind. Ralph was not the *cause* of that event, though he had been her inspiration.

The important thing to note at the end of the scene is simply that she knows. If I am right, the other problems and obstacles in her life will start to fall in place "within" that knowledge ("that knowledge"—the "light," or the new form of consciousness). The basic motion of the plot, i.e., or the change in Isabel, in *The Portrait*, is from ordinary to extra-ordinary, or transcendental, consciousness in the sense that her experience of recognition reveals a greater Self that is capable of regulating proportions and directions of her life on the basis of a total involvement with nature and its forces.

These developments in Isabel support the theory that (1) the central tendency of Henry James (it appears in *The Ambassadors* as well as in numerous other works) is to depict evolving consciousness; (2) if a character achieves the form of consciousness that is the goal of such growth, or if we can regard that form of consciousness as a light, the character's priorities fall into an orderliness (as in St. Augustine) with respect to the light; (3) Isabel turns away from darkness and moves toward the light as if the change itself were her fate.[5] Thus in *The Portrait*, as well as in *The Ambassadors*, one finds the main character's problems with erotic love, desire in general, or such choices as marriage, "mastered" by underlying or overarching insight and knowledge gained in transcendence.

In the final scene, because of this discovery of a transcendent Self, Isabel is on her way to being, literally, no longer at odds with Gilbert, just as she is no longer at odds with the rest of the world around her because she has a "center of gravity." It is no longer *her* fate in confrontation with anyone's at all because she has found the center of her relationship to all things in herself— in her thoughts and in the silence beyond her thoughts which is the source of thought.[6] This region beyond her thoughts is a level of consciousness that will eventually be more clarifying, more enlightening, more illuminating, and more orderly to her than what is transmitted to her from without by others.

Because of the tendency of James to examine the "evolution" of a character's consciousness, one might expect, since the revised *Portrait* contains two transcendence scenes plus a definite change in the heroine, to find in the text a specific explanation for Isabel's rejection of Caspar and her return to Gilbert. In addition, one looks for a hint beyond that last scene even or a promise about the events of her future even though information is lacking on the subject in the book itself. But before attempting a response to such a concern, let us turn to the second transcendence scene.

James often approaches a scene with a characteristic foreshadowing that predicts the scene itself in advance. He opens by showing Isabel at Gardencourt in the garden. She sits on a bench alone; the area has many memories. At this moment, says the author, she is "a victim of idleness." She begins the restful state James so often establishes for moments of transcendence. "Her attitude had a singular absence of purpose; her hands hanging at her sides, lost themselves in the folds of her black dress; her eyes gazed vaguely before her" (Norton ed. 485).

After Caspar arrives on the scene she begins that paradoxical mixture of complete awareness and the slowing down of motion one

---

[5] I use the terms "light" and "darkness" here in the sense of the traditional metaphor of knowledge and ignorance—not to be confused with another use of it that I make on p. 78, i.e., "inner light."

[6] This is not self-centeredness because eventually the self becomes fully identified with nature. This point will be elaborated upon in connection with *The Ambassadors*.

finds in meditation—a "wakeful, hypometabolic physiologic state" (Wallace). She "listened to him as she had never listened before; his words dropped into her soul. They produced a sort of stillness in all her being" (487).

When Caspar says she doesn't know where to turn and asks her why she should go back to Gilbert, she gives her reply, "To get away from you!" and silently recalls to herself that she had never loved before. "She had believed it, but this was different, this was the hot wind of the desert . . . it lifted her off her feet . . . it forced open her set teeth" (488). If Isabel ever felt passion, it was now. And if she were ever to surrender to a lover, it would be now; but we can also see, through Caspar's arrival itself, and increasingly as he talks, that in starting to surrender to Caspar Isabel is also surrendering to something else mentioned above: the "stillness," or the "singleness of purpose." These two elements of experience occur at the same time in her mind and intensify as the scene goes on; for example, as to the passion:

> Isabel gave a long murmur, like a creature in pain; it was as if he were pressing something that hurt her.

And again, the surrender:

> The world, in truth, had never seemed so large; it seemed to open out, all around her, to take the form of a mighty sea, where she floated in fathomless waters. She had wanted help, and here was help; it had come in a rushing torrent. I know not whether she believed everything he said; but she believed just then that to let him take her in his arms would be the next best thing to her dying. This belief, for a moment, was a kind of rapture, in which she felt herself sink and sink. In the moment she seemed to beat with her feet, in order to catch herself, to feel something to rest on. (489)

With the phrase, "the next best thing to her dying," she associates death with a kind of rapture, a feeling of sinking into a sea where the silence, the peace, and the freedom of it end the world's turmoil. I am referring here to the real desire some people have for death; they see it as something to look forward to. I do *not* think that Isabel wants to "escape," in the sense of running away from life. Hers is a desire for fulfillment, and it happens in this scene to be parallel to the experience of transcendence, which also ends in peace, stillness, and an end to turmoil. Her experience is thus a profound spiritual one, but that does not end the complications. In this particular scene, both these experiences are obviously associated with sexual passion. Certainly the passage describes, first a woman who probably for the first time in her life realizes, feels, and up to a certain point knows the overwhelming power of sexual love (in a far more overwhelming sense than with Gilbert)—and the experience that provokes the feeling is with a man she now knows she *could* love.

So she is experiencing two things that remind her of the longing for death: sexual passion, and the attraction of "silence" which is a beginning of transcendental consciousness. Both provide a lure that asks her to surrender. The passage continues: "Ah be mine as I am yours!" she heard her companion cry. He had suddenly given up argument, and his voice seemed to come, harsh and terrible, through a confusion of vaguer sounds. The next sentence seems ludicrously stilted in the middle of a love scene. Yet, when one reflects on the quality of the passages and the conviction of Isabel's thoughts and words at the culmination of this novel, it is clear that there is nothing accidental about the placing of the sentence. The sentence is: "This, however, of course, was but a subjective fact, as the metaphysicians say: the confusion, the noise of the waters, all the rest of it, were in her own swimming head" (489). Henry James added the word "swimming" in the later version. To my mind he wished to re-emphasize the first part of the overall meaning of the passage, that is, he wished to magnify the intensity of activity (to the point of confusion) on the First Level of consciousness. What he has not quite said in the sentence, but certainly implied, is the other side of the coin: opposing the "subjective fact" is the "objective principle." Something else, something like an objective principle of law—as in *The Critique of Practical Reason* where Kant says in effect that the subjective principle of action must conform to the objective principle of law (97–117)—exists which is objective and real, and apparently is more important than the "subjective" fact. The next sentence in both versions reads: "In an instant she became aware of this"—not just aware that all this confusion is there, but also, something else is there. That something is an objectivity whose meaning we can understand more fully after the second version where James fortifies the whole passage as a statement of transcendence. It would not really be clear that this passage is about a transcendent experience just from the second version itself, but by the time that version appeared, James had completed *The Ambassadors*. From the many passages in it depicting transcendence, we can see that James now knows explicitly what it is to transcend (and indeed has now portrayed the experience in his work); and he knows transcendence involves the kind of objectivity he has alluded to in the earlier version of *The Portrait*. With the original use of that term in the first version, James apparently was merely speaking philosophically; now he can show the *experience itself* through a dramatization of transcendence.

The passage is quoted and then discussed in this chapter. First, however, we must detour for a few lines and glance at what Isabel means when she says: "Do me the greatest kindness of all . . . I beseech you to go away." She has begun to know what it means to want him, physically, sexually, and she knows the help in "rushing torrents" that he could offer her in this and so many other respects. Therefore, since she has begun to relent completely and irresistibly to the passion she had feared, she has faced the fear; in fact, the feeling is so pleasant that there is no fear. In the revised version James has taken pains to underscore this point by adding another sentence a few lines later: "She felt each thing in his hard manhood that had least pleased her, each aggressive fact of his face, his figure, his presence, *justified* in its intense identity and made one with this act of possession" (Norton ed. 489; emphasis mine). There is nothing left but to surrender to him (nothing except a surrender to a new form of consciousness). And when, in the next instant, she turns Caspar away, she does not reject her experience with him. He has been her friend as well as her lover, and her tone with him is soft, beseeching, and tearful.

The paragraph from which the new sentence above was quoted contains what are probably two of the most interesting revisions James made in the later edition—in addition to the part already quoted. Now in her experience of transcendence, in the paragraph quoted next, I have italicized the parts James added. The revised version shows the shock—even the ecstasy—of the kiss; but again, the two elements are in contrast; one reveals her recognition of the physical-sexual act, and the other reveals her experience of self-realization, which is complete and clearly identifiable:

> He glared at her a moment through the dusk, and the next instant she felt his arms about her and his lips on her own lips. His kiss was like *white lightning, a flash that spread, and spread again, and stayed; and it was extraordinarily as if, while she took it she felt each aggressive fact of his face, his figure, his presence, justified of its intense identity and made one with this act of possession. So had she*

*heard of those wrecked and under water following a train of images
before they sink.* But when darkness returned she was free. She
never looked about her; she only darted from the spot. There
were lights in the windows of the house; they shone far across
the lawn. In an extraordinarily short time—for the distance was
considerable—she had moved through the darkness[7] (for she saw
nothing) and reached the door. Here only she paused. She looked
all about her; she listened a little; then she put her hand on the
latch. She had not known where to turn; but she knew now.
There was a very straight path. (Norton ed. 489–90)

The most important addition is the white lightning image. This
addition shows a strengthening of the image of a mind approaching
and achieving transcendence. (For purposes of comparison I have
placed the earlier version of the same paragraph in a footnote
below.)[8] In the period between the first and second versions, James
composed *The Ambassadors*, and the effect of that novel on his
development can be seen in the later version of *The Portrait*. The
whiteness Isabel sees when Caspar kisses her is transmitted violently.
Compared to the ordinary light of day, such light has absolute
intensity. Whatever is happening to her physically at this moment,
Isabel is being penetrated or violated by the power of this light,
and James adds to the original paragraph a modifying phrase, "[it]
spread and spread, and stayed," to indicate the expansion of the
light's power throughout her consciousness and the fact that the
illuminated consciousness, because she will always remember the
awareness she felt this day, is here to stay. (In Chapter I of this book,
James describes his experience of the increasing illumination of his

---

[7] This term is one I believe is intended to describe physical darkness. Since
she knows there were lights in the windows, she is not *merely* describing the
darkness that is at the end of the day, because she saw *nothing* (yet the lights
were there). What she is talking about is the blankness, the absence of sense
experience, of transcendence, which can seem like "darkness." To clarify an
apparent contradiction: sometimes seconds after such darkness, the meditator,
or transcender sees an *inner* light.

[8] "He glared at her a moment through the dusk, and the next instant she felt
his arms about her, and his lips on her own lips. His kiss was like a flash of
lightning; when it was dark again she was free. She never looked about her;
she only darted away from the spot. There were lights in the windows of the
house; they shone far across the lawn. In an extraordinarily short time—for
the distance was considerable—she had moved through the darkness (for she
saw nothing) and reached the door. Here only she paused. She looked all
about her; she listened a little; then she put her hand on the latch. She had
not known where to turn; but she knew now. There was a very straight path."
(New American ed. 544).

own understanding of growth to wider and wider circles involving the realization of more and more "sources" and "treasures.") In the next comparison that follows in the quotation, this expansion conveys her feeling of being shipwrecked and sinking into the sea. Her old mind, her old geography, has been shattered by sudden realizations. She sinks, or as it would be in the case of a meditator, her mind settles down (and incidentally, feels as if it is falling), getting ready to "touch bottom"—a phrase James uses frequently in *The Ambassadors* as the end-point of a number of different mental experiences leading to extreme clarity.

From the moment that sinking stops, she is in darkness. From the beginning of the darkness until she puts her hand on the latch, she saw nothing. There *were* lights in the windows of the house, and they *did* shine across the lawn, yet the author reports, "she saw nothing." It had grown dark outside while they were talking; the only way she could have seen nothing while in the darkness of night crossing a lawn and walking toward lights in the house windows would be if her eyes were closed as in sleepwalking *or* if the mind was so totally absorbed with something that the "something" shut out ordinary vision. As soon as she clutched the latch, she came out of her absorption and saw the lights of the house. Her inner vision stopped and her outer vision turned on.

She accomplished this period of darkness in a very short time, even though the distance was considerable. (Since transcendence is beyond sense experience, it is also beyond time, and this explains why hundreds of meditators, after coming out of meditation, often notice that thirty minutes seem like one second.) Again during the time she is in darkness, she is, says James, "free." I am concerned only with freedom in her mind, not freedom from outward limitations such as the grasp of an ardent lover; the feeling of freedom is one of the most common experiences reported by meditators.

All these experiences present evidence of transcendental consciousness, a fact that is enhanced by the late additions. She has one more experience that meditators often have (it appears in both versions), and involves her condition before and after the meditation proper: before, she "had not known" where to turn, "but she knew now." And obviously, when James follows that remark with, "There was a very straight path," he means she's thinking of the rest of her life. She has somehow realized, in that brief space of time, the fundamental direction of her life, which she did not know before. Such an achievement is not likely to have happened in "ordinary" consciousness. For it to happen that fast takes the small bolt of lightning just described.

If we understand what happened to Isabel (following a feeling of passion *and* a vague death wish), then we understand that her choices in the future will be according to the best (in the real sense of the word this time), the most favorable elements and the most perfect "unconscious skills," as Blackmur calls them (*Portrait*, Dell ed.).

We are not told what will happen in her relationship with Gilbert, but, given the nature of her discovery, her *fate*, we can speculate on that subject without being totally arbitrary. If Isabel is transcending, then she has developed, or is on the way to developing, a vision of possibilities that simply were not there, were not available previously. It becomes no longer necessary for her to shuttle between a fixed set of options, as she had before, because her *motivation* is not the same. Consider, for the moment, how one might have interpreted this final scene lacking any idea of her transcendent capability. Her rejection of Caspar might be called simply an avoidance of sexual contact: fear. The result would be a rejection of Caspar as an evasion. A more complex version of this idea (Norton ed., 617) would be that Isabel fears giving in to an erotic attachment because it might cause her to lose her independence and freedom and this is probably correct as far as it goes. But both theories fail to stipulate whether Warburton or Caspar or both would exert this influence over her apart from her *fear* that they would. Both omit the possibility that Isabel could undergo a radical change and lose such a fear.[9] Both also omit the possibility of a total change in the motivation of Isabel, not to mention a motivation with positive consequences. And of course they assume—with quite some evidence on this score—that a return to Gilbert would be a return to a miserable and very likely unworkable situation.

In order to continue to discuss Isabel's future I must make assertions about transcendence that will not be fully developed until later, but they have to be given here to make my case for

---

[9] Fear and transcendence are mutually exclusive. During meditation, as the mind moves toward transcendence, fear diminishes more and more until it completely disappears. As one transcends again and again, as one progresses, what happens during the transcendence of meditation happens more and more in active life. (I am assuming that Isabel, of course, achieved transcendence spontaneously, which does happen—that is, without the benefit of meditation.)

Isabel. If Isabel is on her way to the achievement of a permanent transcendent condition; if she is in the process of shifting to a constant state of self-realization, which is the ultimate situation for someone whose consciousness has been moving as the plot of The Portrait has shown her to be moving (the same directional motion takes place in The Ambassadors), then she not only will in time acquire a different "attitude," "point of view," or "approach to life" but she—her consciousness—will become something like a field of electrical energy that affects those with whom she interacts in a different way than before, automatically. Her approach would be such (call it "so positive") that others would see, even if only preconsciously, that the same old reactions won't work any more or simply won't be needed. To carry this conclusion one step further, the positive field emanating from Isabel would even affect the consciousness of others, including Gilbert Osmond, in a fundamental way. Their reaction would be part of a more subtle interaction than speech or activity, but not magical, and not supernatural. It occurs through the physiology and psychology (see end of Chapter VII) and the latter, in transcendental consciousness, functions on a much subtler level than it does when the person is in ordinary consciousness. An example: after her awakening in the drawing room scene in Chapter 40, Isabel demonstrates a consciousness that differs in a subtle way from any she has displayed before. Her mind finds itself functioning beyond its usual patterns— beyond the level of speech. At the same time she realizes in the environment events or details she has never noticed before. The change continues in the recognition scene in Chapter 42, with her expanding experience acting as a proving ground for the later illuminations in the final scene with Caspar. The original recognition might have taken less than a second, yet the accumulating revelations of Isabel that follow grow deep and strong enough to affect her and the whole of a small community around her.

In the beginning Isabel and Strether did everything backwards. They both had the task of finding out which attachments were "virtuous" and which weren't and why. Their standards, speaking in general, were puritanical, and their method was to manipulate others as well as themselves. In both instances no solution was possible until they discovered a certain new level of consciousness. In neither case did the solution turn out to be primarily acting upon (or rejecting or accepting) someone or something—outside, in the environment. Nor was it accepting an idea. It was a shift in the structure of the mind: once the new consciousness was there, the solution changed because the manner of perception had changed. Isabel refused the comfort of lusty Goodwood, not through fear of any negativity but because of the magnet-like attraction of higher love. When, after the final scene, she returns to Rome and Gilbert, the situation will change because *she* has changed. Strether, after reversing himself completely on the question of what attachments were virtuous, refused the "comfort" of all his friends and associates at home in Woollett and will pay the price when he returns not wearing his old limiting shoes. Also, he gracefully sidestepped Maria Gostrey, and in doing so symbolically sidestepped all fixed attachments of any kind and, like Isabel, abandoned himself to that same higher love.

Isabel, in starting out, was endowed with an imagination and the opportunity to experiment with it in any way she wished. Her problem was that she took her ideas of what is "best" from others and tried to guide her life into the conceptions they collectively formed. When the time came to choose a husband, she betrayed a shrinkage of the imagination that brought her far short of her potential:

the finest—in the sense of being the subtlest—manly organism she had ever known became her property. (Norton ed., 358)

After she went through her trial and self-realizations, she found an internal freedom. Then she was capable of facing the same situation with a difference: this time her own center of consciousness was the starting point.

*   *   *

In a similar manner Lambert Strether's center of consciousness was going to be the starting point, and eventually the end-point, of a long search when he first discussed virtuous attachments with Bilham and Miss Barrace. In his most recent visit with Marie, which we were discussing at the beginning of the chapter, Strether has recognized Mme. de Vionnet, he tells Miss Barrace, as "a tremendously brilliant capable woman" and has started to trust her. In his conversation with Bilham shortly afterward, he says about the affair, "It can't be vulgar or coarse." Bilham echoes: "It can't be vulgar or coarse. And bless us, it *isn't*" (174; 6, II).

The context of these remarks provided by the surrounding conversation, strongly implies that Bilham does not mean his deception to be harmful but actually helpful: "It's, upon my word, the very finest thing I ever saw in my life, and the most distinguished." And Strether admits that she has "saved" Chad. "It strikes you accordingly, then, as for *you* . . . to save *her*," replies Bilham, nudging Strether toward her. His idea is for Strether to learn to appreciate the Countess free of his prejudice about the physical side of the relationship and perhaps come around to his and Chad's idea of what virtue can be. For Bilham's plan corresponds to Chad's, except that, for Chad, the motive for withholding the full truth from Strether is stronger and plainer. He says to his older friend and visitor:

> All I ask of you is to let her talk to you. You've asked me a lot about what you call my hitch, and so far as it goes she'll explain it to you. She's herself my hitch, hang it—if you really must have it out . . . she's too good a friend, confound her. Too good, I mean, for me to leave—without . . . my arranging somehow or other the damnable terms of my sacrifice. (148; 5, III)

As for Strether, the question of the "virtuous attachment" of his two friends constitutes a mental obstacle; his "sessions" with Marie could ultimately make it possible for him to dissolve the obstacle, as I will show (Chapter V), but not before it precipitates the major crisis of the book.

Up to the point where Strether, in the river scene, is confronted with inescapable, irrefutable evidence of the true nature of the attachment, he had what James calls in the Preface a "moral position"; through "rapid, inductive steps, it proved 'false'" (6). As his eyes became opened to Paris, his awareness was wonderfully enlarged; yet up to the last moment his notion of proper sexual behavior remained steadfast, inured to the old geography. That geography opposed St. Augustine, because it said that in a relationship between lovers, good (virtue) "equals" sexual abstinence; evil (sin) "equals" carnal love.

After Strether learns of the intimacy, he is understandably shocked: alas! a wonderful, exemplary woman and a dear friend have been involved in a tawdry sexual affair. After this, *because she is his friend*, he pays Mme. de Vionnet a visit. Once in her presence he finds that, in spite of his temporary shock, nothing in his recent attitude has changed: "she was as much as ever the finest and subtlest creature, the happiest apparition it had been given him, in all his years to meet" (342; 12, II). And as to his feelings for her:

"once more, and yet once more, he could trust her. That is, he could trust her to make deception right. As she presented things, the ugliness—goodness knew why—went out of them" (337; 12, I).

During the succeeding chapters of the novel, from his last conversations with Bilham and Barrace mentioned previously until now, nothing has been said either by Strether or by the author for the reader's sake about his "old" sexual attitude. No explanation has been given for how he might have unraveled the knotted threads he thought he saw.

It is possible for one to think Strether's high opinion of Marie has been shattered, in spite of these last remarks, because underneath it all is "the weight of her sin": (1) she deceived him, (2) she is having sexual relations out of wedlock, and (3) technically, she is an adulteress. But do these remarks by Strether, ending with an endorsement of the virtue of the affair, sound like a disapproval or a condemnation? He departs to seek out Chad and tell him if he does not stay on with Marie he will be guilty of "the last infamy" (354; 12, IV). Actually, Strether has acted according to what he had believed increasingly all summer. As the new information about the deception they had practiced came up against what he now felt about life and intimate relations between lovers, he found the time for choosing suddenly thrust upon him. He was able to make the decision, as I will show in Chapter V, in terms of a "revolution" of his consciousness. He is, at the time of choosing, equipped, thanks to help from the lady herself in the past few months, with a perspective that can circumscribe (in the sense of containing) the "deception" incident in a wider vision, as if he were able to view the earth in orbit after viewing it previously from ground level.

> He perceived soon enough at last that, however reasonable she might be, she wasn't vulgarly confused and it herewith pressed upon him that their eminent "lie," Chad's and hers, was simply after all such an inevitable tribute to good taste as he couldn't have wished them not to render. (337; 12, I)

Thus the deception has been turned into something else, based on an entirely new kind of awareness.

One of the interesting things about *The Ambassadors* is that there are no villains, if we take the theory in this chapter seriously that Bilham, and even Chad, in "manipulating" Strether for Chad's aims, were also trying to prove to him that a different way of seeing things that has a validity of its own, is really possible. Having no villains would be entirely appropriate for a work if its intention is to create a mind so enlightened that it is compatible with the most refined stimuli and responses the universe can offer. If something like that has happened to Strether's consciousness, that could explain how he might recognize that through something in their love affair, even perhaps their intimacy, his two friends have gotten a taste of that larger consciousness that *he* now knows; they have found some part of "well-directed love," or the "Will of the Father,"[10] in spite of the fact that their affair breaks all the rules of conventional morality.

As for Isabel, her path goes in a direction Ralph would approve, just as Strether's at the corresponding point goes in a direction Marie and Gloriani would approve. Both protagonists have struggled painfully with a negative influence, Isabel with Gilbert, Strether with Sarah as she represents Mrs. Newsome and the Woollett bunch. For Isabel to accept Goodwood, along with the "comfort" he offered, would be comparable to Strether accepting Gostrey along with the comfort he knew *she* could offer (something out of it all for oneself). Pansy corresponds to Bilham. Both are young people. Pansy admires and loves Isabel, and Bilham admires Strether so much he wants to be just like him. Finally, from the start, Strether, figuratively, has been headed for Rome even when he was returning to Woollett, while Isabel figuratively and literally headed for Gilbert, and to quote from Isabel herself: "Deep in her soul—deeper than any appetite for renunciation—was the sense that life would be her business for a long time to come" (Norton ed., 446; 53).

---

[10] A more precise term in this study would be Second Level Consciousness.

THE DOUBLE CONSCIOUSNESS

I

The "double consciousness" of Strether mentioned early in the novel[1] is partly the result—as he himself has said—of the inability to keep his mind on the issue at hand ("there was a detachment in his zeal and a curiosity in his indifference"), and partly the result of a conflict of impulses and duty or of sensibility and moral doctrine, contrasts that are familiar to critics who have addressed Strether's problems. These terms describe a common dualism found in American culture and other cultures as well. But the "double consciousness" I refer to in this chapter consists of a wholly different set of opposites. In his later, transformed, condition, Strether achieves the two levels I have been referring to as the "First" and "Second" Levels. In this chapter, I will demonstrate how these two function in the mind of the hero in a concrete sense, eventually uniting and making possible the "realized man" Strether becomes. The double consciousness is the key to understanding the whole intention of the novel. Having shown how it functions (Part I), I will then consider (in Parts II and III) how this development sheds light on the highly dramatic final scene with Marie de Vionnet in Book 12.

In his second visit with Marie at Chad's in Book 4 (167; III), Strether takes a step beyond ordinary consciousness in terms of the

[1] "He was burdened, poor Strether . . . with the oddity of a double consciousness" (18; 1, I).

kind of thinking he usually engages in. Standing before him, the Countess offers an array of qualities; though the author arranges them in contrasts, Strether at first does not see the pairs as contrasting opposites (i.e., he sees A & B, not A *vs.* B); consequently they seem practically meaningless. He sees: "a poet both mythological and conventional"; a "goddess" *and "femme du monde"*; a lady with "a law of her own" who is also a "multifarious Cleopatra"; someone who is "obscure one day [all depth]," "uncovered" the next [all surface]. "'You see how I'm fixed,'" her eyes say to him across the dinner table, "yet how *he* was fixed was exactly what he didn't see" (168). As we get into the dialogue, contrasts multiply; his bewilderment increases. She asks him to trust her when his whole mission (and she knows it) is based on precisely the opposite attitude. Then she asks that he trust *himself*—as though she could tell, as she undoubtedly could, that he was underdeveloped in the matter of trusting people like her.

Within a few moments his mind opens to the possibility of a solution to this confusion. Within the contrasts, certain values appear to be similar. They line up on one side, the underside, of a coin, so to speak; the others line up on the top side. The opposed qualities of "depth" and "surface" offer a kind of key to the rest of the pairs. The underside values are: the "mythological poet"; the "goddess"; the "mysterious law"; and the obscurity or depth. The underside qualities imply a creative power, a permanence, and a potential self-awareness that as a whole contrasts with the changing, worldly, glittering, conventionally-bound values of the other, opposed, items in the pairs. Thus one side of the coin represents, in a particular sense, certain capacities that he discovers as his mind opens to the light of transcendence. And the two-sided representation begins to hint that the final answer might lie in a balance of these opposing forces.

This is especially true in the last opposition that comes up. In the dialogue that follows, the beckoning phrases of the Countess turn on the notion of trust, as Strether openly surrenders to the recently discovered "depth" side of himself. Perhaps it is because this happens in the scene, which is in dialogue, that the author does not explicitly give us a term opposing trust. The obvious one is mistrust, and certainly he overcomes a great deal of that in this one scene, in his surrendering to, trusting, her. But it could be more complex. If Strether discovered a trust in Marie, it would be based on his own immediate experience. Opposed to this would be his earlier beliefs, consisting of a strong sense of duty based not so much on direct experience as on abstract doctrines transmitted through his New England puritan background.

At any rate, once he trusts her, he finds himself "more closely connected" to himself—to his deeper layer—and to the world around him. He has experienced more than he knows, because, as he says, at the moment of realization he was "tripped up," and he "had a fall" (171; 6, III). The "fall" resembles the process of transcendence (described in Part II of this chapter). He "falls" *to* the deeper ("lower") side of the mind. Whether or not Strether could yet describe it in words, his newly discovered side harbors a certain kind of thinking and a certain kind of being, a fineness of consciousness that in its depth, its profundity, is opposed to another part of his mind that harbors another, more obvious "surface" kind of thinking and being. He has not completely found the Second Level of consciousness, but he has a limited awareness that two levels, not only separate but contrasting, exist within him (*that* potentiality of his own mind had to be in evidence in order for him to recognize it in hers). And he may even see that both levels are important aspects of one comprehensive system in his mind.

There does seem to be a compartment in Strether's mind which, by its very nature, agrees with such a compartment in hers, and she does, in part, cause him to recognize this. To do so she uses a lure (171): it amounts to never opposing; she leads him to the edge of precipices, then suggests, with a nod, "Jump." In the scene we are discussing, he senses it is to himself he would be jumping, and indeed, he surmises, this might not be so bad. She asks if Chad doesn't perpetually make her "present" to him (talk about her), to which he replies, "Never." "But," she says, realizing something, "do you need that [Chad's reassurances about her]?" "I see what you mean," Strether replies. "Of course you see what I mean," she says. And it is as if she also says: "You don't need him because you can trust *me*." Strether obviously agrees with her, and with this she has caught him into admitting his trust. Whereupon the author comments, "Her triumph was gentle . . . she had tones to make justice weep" (170).

At this point they get into a discussion of Jeanne, Mme. de Vionnet's daughter. The Countess remarks that he should not only trust her (the Countess) but trust himself as well. Then she more or less gives up on trust. "I'm glad at any rate you've seen my child." This phrase precipitates an extremely dramatic moment. Remember, his problem is lack of trust. Suddenly he comes out with, "She does you no good," and, startled, the Countess says, "No good? Why, she's an angel of light." Strether: "That's precisely the reason. Leave her alone. Don't try to find out [whether she is fond of anyone in particular, and who it is]. I mean . . . about . . . the way she feels."

"Because one really won't?"

"Well, because I ask you, as a favor to myself, not to. She's the most charming creature I've ever seen . . . . Therefore don't touch her—don't want to know. And moreover—yes. You won't." As a result of this speech, the Countess is quite overwhelmed. "I shan't know then—never. 'Thank you,' she added with peculiar gentleness as she turned away."

The phrase that meant so much was simply the "Thank you." Recall that the author describes that leaping over, as I mentioned, as it happens to Strether internally:

> The sound of it lingered with him, making him fairly feel as if he had been tripped up in a fall. In the very act of arranging with her for his independence he had, under pressure from a particular perception, inconsistently, quite stupidly, committed himself, and with her subtlety sensitive on the spot to an advantage, she had driven in by a single word a little golden nail, the sharp intention of which he signally felt. He hadn't detached, he had more closely connected himself. (171)

The earliest description of his experience of "depth" occurred in the introduction to this scene. Here, in the scene itself, Strether has taken another step toward identifying with the deeper consciousness of the Countess. Instead of thinking of the previous speech as someone giving in to someone else, because it is also a form of transcendence to his own deeper consciousness, we can think of it as someone giving in to himself as well. Again, instead of thinking of it as a process of discrimination, we may think of it as merely an involuntary physical motion responding to a force like gravity, because it is not merely a process of "changing his mind"; another, larger mind—still, however, his own—has taken possession.

All of this is happening inside Strether's head, where a lever's click has allowed it to start. He hears a sound ("thank you"). The next thing he knows, he trips, and suddenly he is falling; this means that at the present moment he (his surface mind) is not in control; it is *his* mind not hers, *his* current mental condition, that is "out of control." What is taking control, what he is floating down into, is this other "compartment" of his mind.

In the passage from *The Ambassadors* cited on p. 90, James describes an experience of transcendence—transcendence because it contains a fall, a relinquishing of control, and the reaching of an apparently subtler level. It is Mme. de Vionnet's mind that is subtle here, but his mind is achieving a condition equivalent to hers. And he ends by finding himself "more closely connected."[2] When he *starts*, as an ordinary, conventional man, he believes himself "in control," and then he undergoes a surrender to a larger consciousness. He enters an unknown "place," a place he has been unable to enter before, but in reality a place just nearby, because, as a deeper level of consciousness, it is simply another level of his own mind. The process probably mirrors the author's own thinking in some way and this enables him to describe it for us. Both experiences, the author's (or what we can infer of it) and the character's, correspond to the "meditative model" I described in Chapter II. The model shows how the mind shifts to Level Two and returns, each single session bringing back as from a well a tiny drop of that consciousness that later results in his full change. The net effect shows Strether's initial contrasts being resolved and lends credibility to the conception of Mme. de Vionnet as a teacher leading him toward ultimate self-realization.

II

The second scene that illustrates Strether in transcendence occurs first outside, and then inside, Notre Dame Cathedral (178; 7, I) and continues at breakfast. There are no contrasts and no puzzling bewilderments. It is a study of ecstasy both spiritual and romantic.

Three things are happening: Strether is beginning to speak and react as he sees the world now from the Second Level; he is beginning to recognize more conclusively that two levels, ordinary and extra-ordinary, are revealing themselves in him; and his life is undergoing a "sorting out" as his mind moves toward a synthesis of the levels. Achieving that synthesis would naturally baffle Strether, as was apparent in the earlier Cleopatra scene. In the beginning he understood only as potential qualities[3] the elements of the conflicts he was experiencing: internal self-law, simplicity, stillness, and "a

---

[2] Indicating a closer connection to himself as well as the rest of the cosmos.

[3] That is, he did not think the realization of potential qualities he might have sensed before could ever really happen here, considering his past inadequacies.

sense of safety" (179; 7, I)—qualities of the stabilizing, transcendent side of the meditative model, qualities that he didn't know he had.

Thanks to his unusual friend and instructor, Mme. de Vionnet, he now finds these elements crystallizing and becoming a reality for him. In addition, his mind is surrendering to whatever further changes this bodes for the future. The scene that follows is keynoted by one thought that comes to Strether as he looks up at Notre Dame: "He had the impulse to let things be" (179). Being "full of" existence, he "rests in" existence. He is more content to live in the present—past and future notwithstanding.

Outside the door of the Cathedral are "problems"; inside there are none (179). Inside, the "things of the world fall into abeyance." Inside, he sees a lady (he doesn't yet know it is the Countess) who exhibits "supreme stillness," who is "strangely fixed," in "prolonged immobility,"—all traits that reflect the stable, transcendent, but as yet not fully realized intellect (180), of Strether. She has "lost herself, he could see easily, as he would like to do." She was "one of the familiar, the intimate, the fortunate, for whom these dealings had a method and a meaning," these dealings being meditations in churches and communications about what one does in such situations.

These experiences just referred to—of unworldliness, stillness, "losing oneself in" (180)—of familiarity, intimacy, and happiness— have qualities that meditators report experiencing in abundance in meditation itself as well as in everyday life after practicing medita- tion long enough.[4] In Strether, these qualities announce the pos- sibility of their becoming more fully activated in his consciousness. With repeated transcendence and return to the everyday world, his mind will assimilate these qualities quite naturally. The "picture" re- cently discussed predicts the qualities abstractly, and the later scene that culminates in the passage quoted on p. 90 demonstrates the transcendence in dramatic terms.

---

[4] Bloomfield, Cain and Jaffe report the experience of a five-year meditator: "I remember looking at a tree and feeling so much more how fully alive it was—it wasn't just wood, it was living. I could see the beauty of its creation in every shimmering pine needle, every piece of bark. I had passed that tree many times before, but now it's a fresh perception every time I take a minute to look at it" (174).
An executive who meditates says: "The feeling of reacting against [life] has left, and in its place stands a firmness, growing inner peace, and harmony" (216).

There is no doubt at all that Strether is undergoing a profound change. As he continues to observe Mme. de Vionnet, he gives us an image of her opening a gate and signaling him to enter a world of mystery that extends to infinity: "It was, to Strether's mind, as if she sat on her own ground, the light honours of which, at an open gate, she thus easily did him, while all the vastness and mystery of the domain stretched off behind. When people were so completely in possession they could be extraordinarily civil, and our friend had indeed at this hour a kind of revelation of her heritage" (181–82).

Immediately afterwards he begins to have that revelation: "He felt even as he spoke how at that instant he was plunging . . . " (182), and a moment later, when they sit down to breakfast, "for an hour, in the matter of letting himself go, of diving deep, Strether was to feel that he had touched bottom" (184), and the touching, in that it is transcending, indicates his finer awareness is opening up to make room for something new. Then he notices how "the bright clean ordered waterside life came in at the open window." And then Henry James makes the statement: "The sense he had had before, the sense he had had repeatedly, the sense that the situation was running away with him, had never been so sharp as now."

The final step of the scene bears a close resemblance to the "meditative" passage in the previous chapter of the novel (171; 6, III). The later one reads as follows:

> What had come over him as he recognized her in the nave of the church was that holding off could be but a losing game from the instant she was worked for not only by her subtlety, but by the hand of fate itself. If all the accidents were to fight on her side— and by the actual showing they loomed large—he could only give himself up. This was what he had done in privately deciding then and there . . . . To this tune and nothing less, accordingly, was his surrender made good. (185)

Earlier we had the traits of the realized man appearing in the picture, and now we are given a glimpse of the transcendence in the scene by which he realizes such traits.

Readers have been presented with a series of events, begin-ning at Gloriani's and moving forward to the scene just described that portrays a mind increasingly in transcendence. All the sessions point to similar motifs: diving, plunging, falling. Now something different happens. He is apparently beginning to fall in love with the Countess at the same time as he goes on realizing repeated tran-scendences; in fact, sometimes it is hard to separate the romantic experience from the transcendent one. The transcendent passage just noted, beginning "What had come over him," for example, might also be interpreted as falling in love.

A slightly earlier passage in the same scene seems to reflect an infatuation or romance and little else:

> She was romantic for him far beyond what she could have guessed, and again he found his small comfort in the conviction that, subtle though she was, his impression must remain a secret from her. (182)

The same can probably be said for this next passage:

> . . . the mere way Mme. de Vionnet, opposite him over their intensely white table linen, *omellete aux tomates*, their bottle of straw-coloured Chablis, thanked him for everything almost with the smile of a child, while her grey eyes moved in and out of their talk, back to the quarter of the warm spring air, in which early summer had already begun to throb . . . . (184)

Is Strether falling in love? Or is Strether undergoing a "transcendental" change? Or are the two events both happening at once in a mixture of some kind?

Probably Strether is *beginning* to fall in love with Marie, as this and other passages seem to show. For instance, sitting by the river before the climactic boat scene (321; 11, III), he makes remarks like, "if there was a danger of one's liking such a woman too much, one's best safety was in waiting till one had the right to do so." Later he declares that right to have been established. His remarks on this subject are always suggestive, never declarative. The evidence we have from the story as a whole, carefully weighed, says Strether, is close to being in love with Marie de Vionnet; whether he has in fact experienced a strong infatuation or is falling in love, James keeps under his cloak of perpetual ambiguity. But whichever state Strether is in would tend to magnify and intensify his everyday experiences, and that would help us (as its opposite would not) to understand by contrast the nature of the transcendent experience. By "opposite" I am referring to the feeling of passionate love—one form of happiness—in contrast to the experience of transcendence—another form of happiness. The power of the first is related to desire; the power of the second is its freedom from desire, and so at their roots they are quite opposite.

Let us return to the second experience for the moment as an example. The essential "content" of transcendental consciousness is different and separate from that of the active state of consciousness, as I explained. Let us imagine that this "essential content" is something like a light, but as vast as an ocean, present at all times in the mind of a person no matter how fully involved he is in activity at any given time. Though depicted here as just another object of the senses, not to mention a moving one, actually the light does nothing tangible;[5] but it does in effect shine on every part of consciousness. Meditators say that the essential content "witnesses" consciousness. And it witnesses other activity as well, such as ordinary activity.[6] Once Strether has realized the presence of this curious light separate from everything else, he will have taken a most important step in the development of his "two natures," or two consciousnesses, the active and the silent or witnessing one. In short, alongside his active mind has begun to develop this "compartment," this plane of existence I have been alluding to for several paragraphs. Though he cannot speak to it exactly or manipulate it, he nevertheless is able to maintain a distance from ordinary (active) consciousness and have a clearer perception of it. To use Henry James's terminology from the immortality essay, Strether has found the "treasure," he has broken through to the "source," and its presence is being felt in his everyday life in Paris and is beginning, in an invisible way, to have an effect on it.

When this stage is completed, *desire* will not absorb Strether's attention to the extent that it is the prime mover of his choices; also, other impressions of events from ordinary life cannot overshadow the presence of the newly discovered Self. In such a condition, one can love his possessions without having possessiveness overshadow the deeper reality of existence. So Strether can be infatuated or in love, but the experience will not, to the extent that he is enlightened, overshadow the constant equilibrium provided by his self-realization. Many authorities have commented on such an approach to desire and self-realization, but the clearest explanation I know of is to be found in the ancient *Bhagavad-Gita* as interpreted by Maharishi. (He designates the ordinary, active self of thoughts and desires with a small "s"; and larger, transcendental Self with a capital "S"):

---

[5] Pure consciousness is beyond sensory or "tangible" experience.

[6] I use the term "witness," borrowed from the *Bhagavad-Gita*, to connote "watching but remaining objective," and "knowing"—"to know" is an early if not the earliest meaning of the word.

> Once Being is permanently loved as separate from activity,
> a man realizes that his Self is different from the mind which
> is engaged with thoughts and desires. It is now his experience
> that the mind, which had been identified with desires, is mainly
> identified with the Self. He experiences the desires of the mind
> as lying outside himself, whereas he used to experience himself
> as completely involved with desires. On the surface of the mind
> desires certainly continue, but deep within the mind they no
> longer exist, for the depths of the mind are transformed into the
> nature of the Self. All the desires which were present in the mind
> have been thrown upward, as it were—they have gone to the
> surface, and within the mind the intellect gains an unshakable,
> immovable status. The Self, Being, remains, unshadowed by any
> experience whatsoever. (150)

Two things I have mentioned as essential in Strether's evolutionary path are (1) that separate "compartments" of Self and
activity develop in his consciousness, and (2) that he eventually
manifests his new, transcendent Self on the level of active life. But
how can these two "compartments" be at once together in one's
mind and separate too? I think we need a way of illustrating this
that connects it with our ordinary experience however remotely or
awkwardly. First, we are describing a human experience, not giving
a philosophical definition of an abstract condition. Second, though
one cannot actually discuss the essence of the state of transcendence, because it is beyond space, causation, and time; nevertheless, from experiences given by persons recalling the few seconds
surrounding the entrance into, or emergence from transcendence,
we can get an impression of the impact of transcendence on those
subtle thoughts closest to the experience. Meditators report that
the experience of activity and silence "combined" can be especially
vivid. They undergo something like a deep silence (plus a physical
immobility akin to total restfulness). Yet, at times, if a conversation
starts up within earshot, they experience no change in the silence,
yet *they can hear the conversation.* They experience activity (or noise)
and stillness (or silence) simultaneously.[7] To see how the two poles

---

[7] Though I have touched on these points earlier, I reiterate here for clarification
that it is not too difficult to imagine, in everyday consciousness, such contrasts
as complexity and simplicity, disorder and order, occurring both at once, in,
perhaps, a work of art or a design in nature itself. Yet, they are opposite
qualities, and the fact is simplicity can be separate and distinct from activity;
order can differ and be separate from disorder. And the same is true of activity
vs. stillness. They are all totally separate, yet occur simultaneously and can be

can be further synchronized in Strether, and to what extent, let us turn to the beginning of the novel's denouement, the Lambinet scene in Book 11, III.

The activity of this book of *The Ambassadors*, which culminates in Strether's final visit with Marie, serves as a dramatic example of the "double consciousness" performing in Strether's life as the elements of his consciousness work toward synchronization. For a period of time, a transitional period—in the mind and in the nervous system of an individual developing permanent "Second Level" consciousness—the two levels function parallel to each other, readying themselves for a fusion. In the story, signs of such a fusion are apparent early, as Strether makes remarks like, "I can't separate—it's all one" (312), or, "What I want is a thing I've ceased to measure or understand" (311), and later, "I see it all," he says, as the author has him "fixing on some particularly large iceberg in a cool blue northern sea." It is all beginning, for Strether, to fit together.[8]

I have just shown how Strether learns that the "being-in-love" factor is not the most fundamental one in his relation with Mme. de Vionnet. He has come to know this other identity they are both rooted in as undercutting everything else, so whether he is infatuated or in love or neither, he has an essential stabilizer that no impulse can overshadow.[9] He describes his state of mind just prior to the Lambinet scene, the scene where the "deception" is revealed to him:

---

synthesized, both in nature and in art, and therefore in the mind.

[8] The *Bhagavad-Gita* says: "When once it has recourse to its own nature, the mind stands 'unshaken.' This is Self Consciousness, or pure awareness. . . . From the center of Reality the whole circumference of life is seen to be completely harmonious, for when the center is found, it becomes clear that the innumerable radii all converge from the circumference toward a single point. If the center is not found, then the various radii will be regarded as separate from one another with no common meeting point. This is why the direct experience of pure consciousness [or pure awareness, or pure experience] is stressed" (147).

[9] "Being [pure consciousness] forms the basis of nature. When the mind comes into full unison with Being, it gains the very status of Being and thus itself becomes the basis of all activity in nature. Natural laws begin to support the impulses of such a mind: it becomes as if one with all the laws of nature. The desire of such a mind is then the need of nature, or, to put it in another way, the needs of nature are the motive of such activity. The Self [now] has nothing to do with 'desire and the incentive thereof'" (*Bhagavad-Gita* 284). This explanation has nothing to do with suppressing desire. Desire still functions, but in a different relationship to the Self.

He had the sense of success, of a finer harmony in things; nothing but what had turned out as yet according to plan. It most of all came home to him, as he lay on his back on the grass, that Sarah had really gone, that his tension was really relaxed; the peace diffused in these ideas might be delusive, but it hung about him none the less for the time. It fairly, for half an hour, sent him to sleep; he pulled his straw hat over his eyes—he had bought it the day before with a reminiscence of Waymarsh's— and lost himself anew in the Lambinet. It was as if he had found out he was tired—tired not from his walk, but from that inward exercise which had known, on the whole, for three months, so little intermission. That was it—when once they were off he had dropped; this moreover was what he had dropped to, and now he was touching bottom. He was kept luxuriously quiet, soothed and amused by the consciousness of what he had found at the end of his descent. (320–21; 11, III)

This speech, after which Strether instantly begins preparing his mind for the final visit with the Countess, depicts a restfulness containing, as he says, "a finer harmony in things," "peace," and all things "according to plan." The pendulum has swung out of the world of activity, the "surface mind," to the other component, the "depth mind."

In the first chapter of this book, I said the extra-ordinary or Second Level of consciousness was identified by James through an image of intense light. Let us return to that idea and associate all the qualities of this last side of Strether's consciousness with the one word "light." Some time after this, just after the discovery scene on the river, he has thoughts about a revolution. "On the eve of the great revolution; the sounds had come in, the omens, the beginnings broken out. They were the smell of revolution, the smell of public temper—or perhaps simply the smell of blood" (335; 12, I). In the present story, the cutting edge of the revolution in Strether's mind that he feels so deeply (apart from historical revolutions suggested by this analogy) is the deception of his friends Chad and Marie. The "status quo," the "present regime" of his mind, growing out of the most wonderful experience of his life, has been posited on one premise: the virtue, the *overall* virtue, of his friends, especially Marie because it is she who gave him his "new consciousness." When he learns about it, her deception appears to hurl defiance at every part of his life, including the transcendental condition he has seen developing in himself ever since Gloriani's garden. All that is false, a lie. The result is a supreme insult, a revolt against Strether's entire sense of decency.

But is it really? From beginning to end, a process of revolution has occurred in Strether's consciousness, culminating here with the deception. One could say that revolution, in fact, is the chief preoccupation of the "active" state in Strether. But from beginning to end, the "light" has also been increasing. The revolution and its contrasting silent element, the light, are distinct and separate, but they exist simultaneously. The introduction of two minds, the active and ordinary "confronting" the pure or extra-ordinary, does occur. The deception, or what Strether thought a deception before it disintegrated (with the help of Mme. de Vionnet), did occur. "He could trust her to make deception right. As she presented things the ugliness—goodness knew why—went out of them" (337). But in this case as in the others, the peacefulness also did occur; the silence did occur, the contentment, the orderliness, the fineness, and the harmony as well. Everything that comes under "light" occurred alongside but opposite to the revolution.

I have taken time in the last several pages to isolate and contrast the two states in order to emphasize a fundamental point about *The Ambassadors*. From this juncture in the story, the Second Level of consciousness in Strether is something that should be taken into account in studying *all* of Strether's moves because of its relevance to his perspective and to the vital decisions he makes toward the end. Not to include this factor might result in leaving out the most crucial figure in the whole carpet.

The next step in Strether's growth concerns the integration of two sides. Since we don't yet know the physiological mechanics of a mind integrating, I will use a term that describes what apparently happens: the side represented by the light, the side I have associated with silence, *absorbs* the side that contains active consciousness (involved as it is in revolutions and love affairs and whatever else).[10]

At the opening of Book 12, after the river scene is over and he has made his discovery, Strether might be expected to display a fit of anger. Yet the state of mind which he carefully articulates for us is light years away from that attitude; he is profoundly at ease: "It

---

[10] The description of the meditation model has been derived from interviews with present-day meditators and the description given by the writers of the *Bhagavad-Gita*. The *Bhagavad-Gita* speaks of action being "burnt up": "He whose every undertaking is free from desire and the incentive thereof, whose action is burnt up in the fire of knowledge, him the knowers of reality—call wise" (281).

was an ease he himself fairly tasted . . . . This was a deeper depth than any . . . . " By evening, "his irresponsibility, his impunity, his luxury, had become . . . immense" (334; 13, I). He goes on like this in a kind of revelry of happiness—almost an ecstasy—as a reaction to all that *deception!*[11]

One particular attribute of the new consciousness in Strether that enables him to make such a revolutionary change is what I will call "noninvolvement." Let us assume that a noninvolved person can be both involved and not involved at the same time. It is a paradoxical but quite possible situation. In involvement, to the extent that the senses pull the mind in every direction, they control it. In noninvolvement, the person has achieved a Second Level mentality. If a mind has that ability, the senses do not control it; thoughts have a new referral-point; one sees anew, but at the same time one has a "space" from which to contemplate this original involvement without interruption.

Gradually the person begins to function less by commands from the ego, mind, desire, or intellect bounded by individual needs and concerns, and more by nature as a whole, that is, the laws of nature, which are universal. This process, vital to my argument, will be developed more fully in Chapter VI.

While approaching Marie for his last visit, Strether received a forecast of a "revolution," which I have identified in a personal sense with deception on the part of his two friends. If he had had to evaluate the deception through no other perspective than the one he had before—there is no way he could have perceived Marie as trustworthy and the deception as a "tribute to good taste." On the contrary, probably the perception would have triggered anger (he has been cheated); angry, he would be "involved," that is, have only his singular involvement from which to contemplate things; from anger comes a judgment, *probably* a vindictive one.

The new consciousness affords him a distance from that framework of typical, predictable thinking. It supplies a state of awareness that is "free."[12] Between the time of his mentioning the revolution

---

[11] "When Being first begins to be infused into the nature of the mind, the mind becomes intoxicated with a feeling of self-sufficiency. When the mind in this state acts through the Senses, it behaves in a rather carefree manner" (*Bhagavad-Gita* 340).

[12] "When the lower Self has been mastered by the higher Self, then the two become one. When transcendental consciousness (absolute Being) is in coexistence with the relative aspect of the mind, the mind of the higher Self

and the time of its "absorption," what goes on? During this period, Strether watches Marie as she becomes a symbol to him even while he is reeling from the shock of what he saw on the river just before he resolves the deception problem and just after he mentions the "revolution." She offers a reassurance and an encouragement, not with words but by example. She displays for him, as his thoughts interpret it, *her* double consciousness. While being a "mild deep person," she can at once be a person "committed to movement" (he notices). "The associations of the place—the gleam . . . the subdued light, . . . the glass the gilt and parquet" all contrast with "the question of her own note as center." We have unity in diversity, the disorder of variegated activity contrasted with the order of stillness; we have an outward suggestion, in other words, of an inward consciousness containing two elements, activity and stillness (or "noise" and "silence"); both are real and present; she is "abounding" in both, and she is remarkable for her ability to "bridge intervals"—intervals that bring opposites together. She is really immensely stable.

There is one major difference here between the form of Strether's consciousness and hers. Assume that both minds do contain the levels of consciousness I have been referring to, and both are in the process of integrating, or have integrated, sets of opposites; he is undergoing his experience for the first time; she has undoubtedly been at it for some time in the past, perhaps years. She is a teacher pointing out to a novice (even if only by signals) that "two consciousnesses" can function well together in the same person,[13] and that, in spite of distractions and even deceptions, he need not revert to the old geography.

It is then that it strikes him. The "lie" *was* simply a tribute to good taste. And it is then that he says, "Once more, and yet once more he could trust her. That is, he could trust her to make deception right. As she presented things, the ugliness—goodness knew why—went out of them; none the less too that she could present them with an art of her own, by not so much as touching them" (337).

The qualities of good taste and trust become "active" in him. As to trust, I am not saying he did not know about trust prior to meeting Marie, but that it became fully operative only after he

---

robs the lower Self of its individuality bound by time, space, and causation—and sets it free" (Bhagavad-Gita 330).

[13] See Chapter III of this book, pp. 54–55, where both the process and the evidence of the occurrence are given.

met her. What is the connection between the "operative" aspect and Level Two? With the complete integration of Levels One and Two, Level Two can be considered as "comprehending" Level One, in the sense of encircling, or absorbing it. We know that the mind experiences an increasingly finer level of thought prior to transcending; we know that a personal experience of "oneness with the universe" is at the very heart of transcendental consciousness itself. It is likely that Strether by now has achieved an infusion of transcendence at successive intervals to the degree that, through the refinement and trust his mind can now offer as an accompaniment to the activities of the present world, he can see the full meaning of at least one ordinary experience, the affair of Marie and Chad, in an entirely new light. The declaration he makes (quoted in the previous paragraph) lends strong support to the contention that the comprehending capacity of the Second Level is alive in our hero.

III

The final conversation of Strether with Marie approaches, in a most concrete way, the realization of James's definition of the heart of his novel as given in the Preface, where he says it is a question of stability—stability in the midst of flux.

What is the role the Countess plays in the final scene with Strether? The subjects discussed go everywhere, and in the discussion her emotions sometimes go quite wild. Does it all mean she has dropped the role of goddess (or teacher) and become a "maidservant" broken up about a lover (342; 12, II)? Actually, she plays the same role here as before, that of "goddess" and teacher. All the activity of the discussion does go on, all the probing, all the grief and joy—but the influence of Gloriani, the "extra-ordinary" influence, goes on too, in her as well as in Strether. The difference is now that what they discuss means something in the ordinary sense and something else when examined under the lens of the extra-ordinary, the "Gloriani"—factor.

The violence of it, the revolution, in terms of consciousness, is like a spear hurled directly at the hero's face. The spear will be deflected, melted. Trust will replace mistrust; "deeper" consciousness will encompass "surface" consciousness. But before this transformation, extending throughout his past life and incorporating the influence of generations that cultured his present beliefs, are thoughts about sexual love that he is being forced to re-examine. He has been undergoing a preparation for this moment for some time—for as long as his position on the subject of "virtuous attachments" differed from that of his new European friends. Now he must ask, is sexual love, after all, so "evil"? Or if it is not, the present circumstances force him to ask under what conditions sexual relations can be "good"?

Strether stands in the Countess's drawing room at the opening of the picture scene and assembles a variety of facts. Each fact works for him like a little golden nail, placing him, as it is driven in, closer to his final awareness.

1. He sees that the Countess's greatest concern is to discover whether he has "stood" what he learned in the river scene and not simply given up on her. Even before she saw him he could tell she was fairly certain of this; but now, he says, she wanted to see for herself (337).

2. He could see "that his intervention had absolutely aided and intensified her intimacy" (337). In this instance he would be referring to the closeness of her association, of her friendship, with Chad in terms of their deepest feelings. Strether has indeed been involved all along, and now he recognizes the fact.

3. "In fine, he must accept the consequences of *that*" (337, my emphasis). He sees he definitely has a responsibility to Chad and Marie; he is preparing to confront the meaning of an involvement that is at this point more fully disclosed than at any time before.

4. Besides these new facts, other information about the affair is important: the Countess appears to have had a "civilized" (my term) separation from her husband. A truce is in force at present, but the separation is real and permanent. She has been compatible—more: happy—with Chad for quite a long time. As to the relationship, not one sound of an objection about it comes from the Countess; furthermore, her friends (for example, Bilham and Barrace) know all about the affair and unquestioningly respect the couple's behavior. The arrangement is hardly unique. For generations Europeans have elected to remain legally married even though incompatible with a first husband or partner while living with a second on a permanent basis. Originally this was done so as not to defy Church law, but in many instances it occurred, and still does, simply because of the stigma attached to divorce, or other "legal" reasons, perhaps—the same kind that sealed the match in the first place.

5. The problem of intimacy in relationships is hardly an immediate concern of the Countess at this point; this late in the game she is not agonizing over whether sexual intimacy is right or

wrong or what the neighbors might think. On the other hand, when he goes to see her the day after the river scene, Strether has been in possession of his new information for just about 24 hours. What to think about sexual intimacy in love affairs is an immediate problem for Strether, and it is a problem he has to solve (or finish solving) in his own mind before he can presume to give useful advice to his friends.

6. As he sought the final answer to his friends' problems and his, he would in some way have to mull over different aspects of the problem raised here. He might have speculated: if a couple has feelings toward each other that are as deep, subtle, and loving as theirs, why could not sexual intimacy be but an extension of that same kind of feeling? That speculation would bring him in the range of Augustine's conclusion, that it is the "good-use" or "mis-use" of sex that makes it good or evil, not the mere fact of a relationship—therefore carnal love is not automatically evil but may be the opposite. This point answers part of the dilemma Strether had.

In a more general sense he has become a person whose presence on any scene clarifies the situation because of his perspective, which, contrary to what it was, is now based on an integrated experience of surface and depth mentality, and is therefore, stable. "He had absolutely become, with his perceptions and mistakes, his consciousness and his reserves, the droll mixture of his braveries and his fears, the general spectacle of his art and innocence, almost an added link and certainty, a common priceless ground for them to meet upon (337). The "common ground" phrase has a primary meaning that rather makes Strether into a "territory" where the "outlaws"—his fellow characters—can get sanctuary. The "ground," which is "priceless," like the treasure in his mind, is the depth level of consciousness. To the extent that his surface consciousness, on one end of the mind's spectrum, has become integrated with depth consciousness, which ultimately consists of the total collective force of the natural universe (Chapter VI of this book), he is balanced, or stable. Strether, once a student, is now, himself, in the last scene with Marie, also a teacher and he has become a stabilizing influence for her as she undergoes her own time of being tested, as now, when she needs *his* consolation and wisdom. Thus the phrase "stability in flux" in the Preface refers not merely to the arrangement of events in the novel's structure but also to the structure of the hero's mind, which has achieved stability in a psychological sense as well as a metaphysical one. The *Bhagavad-Gita* comments on such a situation:

> As long as the mind is one-sided, subjected only to activity and without the direct influence of Being, it fails to be a successful mediator. It fails to safeguard the self from the influence of action, and at the same time, fails to safeguard action from the limitations of individuality, so that activity remains without the direct support of the almighty power of Nature.
>
> But if the mind becomes as familiar with Being as it is with activity, it finds itself as the Self, completely unattached to activity, ever remaining in the absolute state, "in happiness," a silent witness of all events, "neither acting nor causing action to be done." (372)

The difference is now that his activity is immersed in that Being, even though it (the Being) remains apart. And it is from this stability, supporting him in this final moment with Marie, that Strether forms his last impression of her and makes the decisions to say what he does about the value of her current affair, all of which is taken up with more finality in my next chapter.

VI

ONENESS OF VISION

A number of critics of *The Ambassadors* are vague about what makes the *positive* side of Strether's change come about. What are the specific instances or involvements in the story that account for such enhanced inner observational powers as Strether finally achieves? For many, the answer to the question is that Strether just happens to be a man with an unusually discriminating mind, and with that mind he pulls himself up from dullness and lack of confidence to be a dazzling, independent and charismatic human being. But even if one says he did it all by conscious deliberation, one must ask, what was behind that? One cannot keep coming back to how smart and discerning he is or we do not have a plot, we have a man with a portable *deus ex machina*. Supposing, then, this change is accomplished through a process of transcendence; and supposing, as a result of transcendence, it is a change of perception: what is the meaning of the change and how does it work? Is it enough to speak of some inexplicable transformation in the hero that takes him beyond rational thought? Is it just something "mystical"? Or again, is it that the hero, as some critics would seem to suggest, was simply inspired by a grand summer in Paris, and the result, the whole personal revolution, is nothing but mildly unusual?

As I have said, it is my contention that the change is due to a transformation in his consciousness that occurs because he discovers a way of pursuing the deeper, unmanifest, or potential, areas of his own mind. This discovery forms the basis of his new perceptual discovery and is in turn based on the process of transcendence mentioned above.

I have run across critics who, acknowledging the change in Strether, assume the new man has somehow eradicated the old one, that the glowing influence of Paris has done away with the gloomy man of "Woollett," or that Strether's European morality completely supplants puritan dogma, as if to say one's past thoughts disappear from the face of the earth when one grows into something new. My reply to this is that all the dualisms, the paradoxical opposites Henry James is so fond of in this novel, remain viable at the end, but regulated and integrated by means of a "common ground" functioning in an atmosphere of transcendence.

One other interpretation that concerns me is the opinion that the final change in Strether, and for that matter several Jamesian heroes, is a product of "renunciation." This may be so in some works earlier than *The Ambassadors*,[1] but in *The Ambassadors*, what might, in the early Strether, a young man of New England conscience, have seemed like renunciation has later been transformed into something different. That is, what is sometimes taken for renunciation in the later Strether is in fact a surrender to his greater self, not a refusal of life because of excessive moral inhibitions or a withdrawal from it because of fear, even if at one time that might have motivated his actions and indeed been his only solution. At this point, he is led or gravitates toward another kind of renunciation—actually a surrender—by a process of transcendence. That is clear from the passage in Notre Dame described in Book 11. Also, the process of surrender to transcendental consciousness is followed by a later integration of transcendental with ordinary consciousness (or with "old reality") and that extra step produces a balanced view of reality instead of an escape into darkness through avoidance of something in life one fears.

The last concern I have involves the nature of Strether's perception. Is it really sufficient to view Strether's method of perception, throughout his change, as the function of a simple subject-object dichotomy? This is the question that I now pursue,

---

[1] For instance, Tony Tanner mentions one: in Madame de Mauve, he says, when a character "almost becomes passionally [sic] involved" with one of the other characters, he (the character) makes a revealing comment about himself: "Why should his first—and last—glimpse of positive happiness be so indissolubly linked with renunciation?" Agreed. A renunciation of sorts probably does occur in this character in "Madame de Mauve" (37).

because the conception one has of Strether's change depends upon the conception one has of his perception in general, and this is especially true in the later stages of his development.

I

Among the questions the story of *The Ambassadors* raises at the end, the two most commonly asked are, why did he not marry Maria Gostrey, and why did he return to Woollett instead of remaining in Paris? Because of what we now know about the change in Strether, particularly with respect to transcendental consciousness, these questions suggest more than they literally ask. Confronted with marriage of any kind, what could be expected of him with his *new* order of consciousness? What other options are there for Strether *now* besides returning to Woollett or remaining in Paris?

If my hypothesis is correct and he is "enlightened," or approximating enlightenment, a plausible definition—but one actually complete enough to be a model of enlightenment—might tell us what is to be expected of him and why he does what he does. I have shown that throughout his Paris visit Strether repeatedly encounters the "source" area that James's immortality essay talks about—that margin of untapped consciousness that became the beginning of his new-found independence and freedom. In the novel, Strether's experience of this source area, "pure" consciousness, is illustrated by the metaphor of the Babes in the Wood (345; 12, III) and by such other passages as the description of "surrender" to Mme. de Vionnet early in the Notre Dame scene. In Chapter II, I described how Strether's first infusion of this pure experience was rendered through the light imagery at Gloriani's and again through the light imagery in the Luxembourg Gardens.

We can see these experiences (of transcendental consciousness, whether they be full enlightenment or not) in the mind of a fictitious character like Strether, and there is also the probability—already suggested—that Henry James in fact experienced transcendental consciousness. Since the time of Henry James, a new body of scientific information has evolved out of which comes a clearer understanding of and a more convincing approach to other experiences people have had of this kind, some of which occurred long before the present era of experimentation began. In the recent experiments, trained meditators have recorded their impressions of the "pure" experience personally. Other experiments demonstrate the objective physiological validity of the experience.

In addition, examples of the occurrence go far back in history; one set of examples goes as far back as the *Bhagavad-Gita* in the Veda of India, a document dated conservatively at 1500–1000 B.C. The authors of this writing were probably the first to recognize and record transcendental consciousness. Their reports, and their accompanying descriptions of an enlightened individual, insofar as it is possible to describe one, provide a model for testing Strether's experiences. I will offer some of these reports in this chapter; if they match Strether's mind favorably, we can not only identify his advanced stage of development but have an altogether new way of understanding him.

One of the most important capabilities of a realized man, according to the *Bhagavad-Gita*, is noninvolvement. In the simplest sense, noninvolvement results from repeated immersions in pure consciousness followed by returns to activity. As fully elaborated in the *Gita*, the experience turns out to be *both* involvement and noninvolvement even though the latter term is used to describe both. Of course, to be involved and noninvolved at the same time seems like a contradiction: the *Gita* says the enlightened man recognizes that he is, simultaneously, in the state of unbounded Being or noninvolvement separate from activity on one side, and involved in the world of forms and phenomena on the other. Meditators, to the extent that they can describe it, say the experience renders a feeling of motionlessness, of silence, and of freedom of thought in the sense that one finds himself not feeling the pressures of life. On the other hand, one also finds himself reacting to his environment and to the thoughts he has about those reactions. (The experience parallels the motionlessness and silence just mentioned).

How do the two apparently opposite functions work together in Strether's mind? Let us return momentarily to the beginning of Strether's experiences with his consciousness as it changes from Level One to Level Two. Take an early session with the Countess, before any of this "involvement-noninvolvement" has developed. Initially, in these learning sessions, Strether's mind would appear to be in motion, and it would proceed toward a point where it would "stop." Obviously, ordinary consciousness is to be identified here with motion; transcendence is motionlessness or "stopping." In the scene in Notre Dame (185; 7, I) Strether says he fully knew the moment at which this first sense of falling, plunging, letting go had taken him; having lost control of his resistance, he, after falling, surrendered to Mme. de Vionnet with respect to this new tendency he has of "going beyond things." After that it is as if he were viewing his own consciousness, watching the motion of his own mind. First, without fully seeing, he senses something to which he knows he will surrender. The experience is at first like "sinking below"; and "the situation is running away from him." But then something other than the Countess's mere charm causes him to stop holding back. Consciousness rushes ("downward") toward transcendence. When transcendence has been reached (and everything appears to stop) "fate intervenes"; Strether says it is all *inevitable*. The description gives us the impression that, once transcended, he could be floating in space; at least he is free from external pressure of any kind. Whatever activity there is in life, at the moment he can rest out there and watch as if life were going on by itself. In most of the novel, whenever he is about to transcend, that sinking or diving is initially determined in the presence of Marie. If he surrenders, he lets the motion take him to her. But, as I have implied, taking the "target" (the stopping place) into consideration and Marie as a metaphor representing that stopping place, it is a motion toward her as a revelation of peace, order, and silence; it is a motion toward "motionlessness." That ordered, silent experience forms (is a verbal approximation of) the *substance* of his separation from activity. What he caught sight of was a "faculty" (it is not merely connected with noninvolvement but may be the essence of it), and that faculty enables him to be outside of, a witness to, everything he does. As I have said, logically the two parts of noninvolvement functioning together appear to be in contradiction; but very simply, the human organism is, after all, in many ways capable of performing two unrelated acts at once—as, for example, listening to music and carrying on a conversation. (I am considering a *stage* of development here. In full enlightenment, Being, the essence of noninvolvement, forms the *continuous* ground from which one acts.)

In his "Project of Novel," Henry James tells us, probably before having completed the novel, what it is that he wants to make Strether come "face to face" *with* in those last visits with the Countess: "He sees and understands, and such is the force in him . . . that he has, almost like a gaping spectator at a thrilling play to *see himself see* and understand" (my emphasis). He is describing the uninvolved condition. In the same passage he expands on the value and scope of this seeing ability. He says he realizes, face to face with her, "what he previously neither really made out for himself nor really dismissed: the strange fact—of an order both obscure and [yet] recorded." And being able to see this in her, he "is in the presence of more things than he has yet had to count with, things by no means, doubtless, explicitly in his book . . . ," i.e., his knowledge (*Notebooks* 410).

For another illustration of this unexpected vision, let us turn to the story itself. As he approaches the end of his journey he sits overlooking a river by an inn. He distinguishes two things: his "prior, restricted state" and the present one in which "their time [his and Marie's] together slipped along smoothly . . . melting, liquifying, into this happy illusion of idleness" (322; 11, II). He is at this moment contained in the limits of his old geography, yet his subterranean thoughts have begun to roam a great distance, gleaning new territory as he drifts into the noninvolved state apart from activity—hers, Chad's, even his own. With this, two new experiences have become noticeable. The first is "melting, liquifying," which suggests his awareness of the interconnectedness of things. The second is his sense of "being"—of simply existing, having substance. He knows that he *is* and he knows that he has a Self. "Don't like me if it's a question of liking me for anything obvious . . . "; he does not want her to like him "for anything he's done for her . . . " but for what he *is*. What he *is*, in the present scene, is immersed in a "melting, liquifying" fluid that underlies his everyday self and yet goes all through him. The commentary on the *Bhagavad-Gita* has a passage describing the same effect. (Imagine Strether's "fluid" as the light of the sun, and that as a purveyor of awareness): "The light of the lamp is invisible to the light of the sun. The glory of the drop has no effect on the glory of the ocean. The joy of an action leaves no lasting impression upon the bliss of [fulfilled] consciousness. Once a man is established in this state, he naturally enjoys so great a fullness of Being that he never feels he is out of it" (342).

Up to now, citing both the *Gita* and the novel, I have represented the noninvolved factor in the hero as if it were something physical. Other features it has are less easy to represent that way. The noninvolved element gives one the ability to observe the activities of the mind as if from a platform, elsewhere as it were. That element also has the ability to "witness" (watch) the platform itself. Thus one is conscious of, or reflecting, activities of all kinds; but in another part, still part of the uninvolved mind, one is not reflecting *on* anything. He is just reflecting (i.e., Self-reflecting); he is not conscious of any particular object. He is just conscious, period.

The next step for the person experiencing all this is to realize that it is really happening; to realize that the double vision of outward and inward watching has become constant; and since wherever he goes it is with him, he now sees everything in the universe in a different way. His vision (like the light) surrounds and contains consciousness at all times everywhere.

II

In the following passage from the Preface to *The Ambassadors*, describing the situation of a writer of stories, James offers a perfect analogy to the situation of the "witnessing" self, and remarks on how a writer, in the act of plying his trade sometimes causes a character to go beyond the ordinary (or beyond what he ever expected); he experiences something he calls "precious," a summit of boundless energy, a self-moving energy, and he claims he gains from it a final kind of knowledge. "There is always, of course, for the story-teller, the irresistible determinant and the incalculable advantage of his interest in the story *as such*; it is ever, obviously, overwhelmingly, the prime and precious thing (as other than this I have never been able to see it); as to which what makes for it, with whatever headlong energy, may be said to pale before the energy with which it simply makes for itself. It rejoiced, none the less, at its best, to seem to offer itself in a light, to seem to know, and with the very last knowledge, what it's about . . . " (6–7).

"The energy with which it simply makes for itself," and with that energy, it "knows with the very last knowledge." The *Bhagavad-Gita* commentary matches this insight exactly: "He [the enlightened person] is firmly secure in existence, which, though the very *basis* of action, is without activity. For him, it is as if everything were going by itself" (341).

In Strether's case, the knowledge is born and instilled in him by the radiance of Paris: "In this most interesting of great cities [Strether] was to be thrown . . . upon his lifelong trick of intense reflexion: which friendly test was to bring him out . . . [to] more things than had been dreamt of in the philosophy of Woollett" (8).

Where the noninvolved factor in the hero's mind starts to be accompanied by the qualities of wholeness, oneness, "is-ness" (Being), and "knowingness" (knowing what it knows),[2] or when

---

[2] The essence of the uninvolved Self, the part which "makes for itself," the part in which one is merely "conscious" as opposed to "conscious of," is the same

an artist is in the act of creating, he seems to be carried away by his work as if it "goes by itself." That is, when the extra-ordinary (noninvolved) factor reveals itself, at that point a surrender in the character to a larger vision is occurring. Indeed, all the qualities mentioned here are qualities produced by transcendence. This is what the Paris experience really is for Strether. It takes him "beyond himself," figuratively, yet in transcending he *literally* goes beyond himself.

Was the experience of transcending then something exclusive? Was Paul's experience on the road to Damascus exclusive or could it happen to anyone? Actually it could happen to anyone. I quote here the discovery of a college student who developed an interest in meditation and practiced it regularly:

> After having meditated for six years, I've noticed that every-thing inside of me has become so much calmer that I interfere less with the larger pattern of whatever is going on around me. I used to have so much inner noise, either emotional turmoil or intense thinking, that I wasn't able to appreciate the larger developments taking shape all around me. As a result, I feel my participation in life now is more an appreciation of what happens in *and* around my life, instead of trying to make this or that happen. I call it "participatory alertness." You find you're maintaining a balance between keeping up active participation to the fullest possible extent and having this continual alertness to a larger awareness of developing situations and patterns so that you aren't caught up in trivia, you aren't forcing things to happen, but you're able to see more clearly at every moment what you can be doing that's most significant.

And another meditator says in the same series of interviews:

> You don't lose a lesser value just because you've gained a greater value. Things keep going on in the world, but the beauty is, when one person is unshakable, then he's better able to stabilize everything else around him just by [his] being who he is, and then his action just augments his being, just increases the effect of that stability by expanding it, by making it available to the environment. (Bloomfield 175–76)

---

entity to which Kant refers when he uses the term "Das ding an sich," the thing in itself. In the Vedic writings, it is the "thatness," the "tat twa m'asi," that which is beyond sense experience yet resides in experience wherever it occurs. An ancient saying from India goes: "I am that, thou art that, and all this is that." It is "in" me, you, and all the environment.

A number of the experiences of Lambert Strether are echoed in these meditators' discoveries: the first meditator finds himself participating in and yet standing back and observing life around him. If he is approaching enlightenment, he has a double faculty of perception that is a definite, known stage in the development of one approaching that state. If enlightened, the experience is constant and the two minds are integrating. He is calmer than in the past and appreciates "larger developments," a greater universe. To the other, "things keep going on, but the beauty is one . . . is able to stabilize everything else around him just by being who he is." The noninvolved factor has become the key to his character, that part which subtly and indirectly affects his relation to others and the part through which he finds himself identifying with nature.

III

Clearly Strether has experienced the phenomenon described here as "witnessing" and his discovery has changed his vision. But how does the experience of transcendence alongside activity make a difference in Strether's perception of specific objects, the growth of perception being what many consider the main theme of the novel? Tony Tanner's article on *The Ambassadors* in 1966 is closer to the "transcendental" approach than any other I have found. In the main, the conceptual model of Strether's process of perception he gives is so clarifying and so accurate that it could be a centerpiece for most of the criticism of *The Ambassadors*. In his discussion of the restructuring of Strether's perception and his examination of the nonparticipating heroes in *The Ambassadors* and other works, Tanner offers the perfect starting place for one to demonstrate the effect of transcending perception.

Tanner says Henry James himself, in his *Autobiography*, "projects an image of consciousness which . . . is . . . increasingly excluded from direct participation in life . . . . " From the start, "mixed with his awe at the boundless wonders of life, was an inner fear of its potential dangers and terrors." *The Ambassadors* became the culmination of a certain type of character, an "appreciative but apprehensive spectator," who evolved throughout the stories and novels prior to that novel. A story like "A Passionate Pilgrim" depicts a character "with a typically Jamesian combination of enraptured yearning for experience of life and a deeper feeling that life itself is fatal to handle." *Roderick Hudson* is an artist stimulated by "a new wealth of experience [experience that is too intense], and later he is betrayed by it." This novel reveals, Tanner says, something about James himself: "He seems to have felt, or dreaded, that the slightest real involvement with the rich stuff of life would prove fatal." In many stories depicting a detached observer, including *Daisy Miller* and *The Sacred Fount*, the main adventure is the character's "own musing, appreciating, evaluating consciousness, but [the character] stays out of the mess of life." (The detached situation Tanner describes is not the same as the "witnessing" one I have been discussing. In the latter, transcendence is a prior condition; in the former it is not. In neither of these last two stories has James brought transcendence into the picture and the "detached" heroes end up very lonely men. In the case of *Daisy Miller*, the message transmitted to Winterbourne by Daisy's death is that, had he been able to commit himself to her obvious affection more openly, the tragedy might never have occurred. The story in Tanner's scheme becomes an argument against too much nonparticipation, and this may be just what it is. Later on in the works of Henry James this detachment becomes something else entirely.

The main implication of Tanner's premise is that in stages throughout his career James had been attempting to perfect a type of observer or nonparticipant, and usually the setting for this development is an avoidance of life that had begun at some point in the character's past. (To many critics the avoidance can be of a potential sexual attachment, but Tanner says it can also be a general apprehension about life's dangers, or of course, both.)[3]

Tanner selects two scenes in the story that characterize the change in Strether's perception. The first is an early scene where, as he approaches Chad's flat for the first time, he stops and finds himself looking at Chad's balcony. "We can regard Strether's progress in Europe as an ascent to a balcony," he says. To Strether, watching from across the street, the balcony seems like a place difficult to approach and not easy to surrender once gained. Strether is pausing "before the whole question of what he might do about Chad" (and that struggle will embrace the struggle with himself and with others

---

[3] I must anticipate myself and contradict the conclusion drawn by Tanner and many critics: Strether's final situation is not "apartness from life." If Strether has achieved a keener appreciation of his senses, he must gain a keener appreciation of reality. And if one accepts that his renewed condition involves a better vision and therefore a keener awareness of reality, (a) he cannot be wholly apart from it, and (b) it is a contradiction to say his new self, with its new perception, was produced by avoidance, or fear, because fear does not improve perception, it distorts it.

that changes his perception). The balcony, Tanner implies, takes on features analogous to the heightened consciousness that Strether will later acquire. The balcony is not only out of Strether's reach physically, but inwardly he seems to feel it is a kind of reality that is beyond him.

In Book 11, shortly before he discovers the illicit relationship of his two friends, Strether stands *on* the balcony and is "in possession as he had never been" (Tanner 41). It is "a possession which is also generous and grateful—non-exploitive," says Tanner. Strether looks *down* now, he has achieved a "perched privacy," and he thinks about his "new precious freedom to enjoy." This, says Tanner, "is a protective place of contemplation from which he can see life but it cannot reach him."

The balcony scenes, first showing the hero "below" and later "above," first "outside," reaching, later "inside" and in possession, give a clear and simple analogue to the general plot as it involves Strether's change of perception. Also, the two scenes represent, respectively, the basic outline of James's early and late "epistemologies" as they unfold in this particular novel. The early one is a typical dualism, consisting of Observer and Object observed, as follows:

(A) Man   sees   (B) Physical Reality
    (observer)   (objects—such as a Balcony or
                                  anything in his environment)

Man, with his ego, mind, and emotions, is "in here"; world is "out there"; perception consists of getting one's mind to make an accurate copy or copies of the "true reality" "out there." But this blueprint only takes perception so far. Thanks to the process of transcendence, Strether develops a more complex as well as a more refined method of perception than this altogether.

Let us turn from the balcony scene a moment and consider, simply, Strether's mind. One can say that in Strether, as a normal human being, the eye takes in impressions which are then imprinted as if on a screen, and these impressions are what the reflecting part of the mind then "operates" on. Strether (to return to the balcony scene) sees the image of life on the screen just as Tanner indicates. As the summer goes on, his mind begins its transforming change. After a period of time, his mind does not see the same thing—or does not see it in the same way—as before. During his second visit, as he mounts the balcony, reality has shifted, as Tanner correctly says, as though having another basis (which it does have), and now his vision has improved, his taste has improved, his enjoyment of everything is greater; he is, in fact, in a superior mental condition— he is more confident and he simply knows more. However, I would go further and point out that the inner nature of Strether's perception has changed. Countless experiments in recent years have shown a change during meditation that gradually becomes pervasive and permanent in the physiology (see Chapter III). The change in Strether as well as in the meditators is a function of transcendence (were we able to test Strether experimentally, the change would also prove to be physiological). The change occurs in the following way:

Let us first bring the description of Strether's consciousness in line with the 1910 essay of James, "Is There a Life After Death?"— analyzed in my Introduction. There, Henry James envisions the operation of perception as almost entirely internal. Consciousness "contains" the world, and it is the equipment we use to apprehend the world.[4] Hence, what we know depends upon the condition of our consciousness. If that condition includes "extra-ordinary" consciousness, once the new factor is integrated with our everyday consciousness the result as a *whole* will determine the kinds of perceptions we make. The mind progresses to that new kind of perception, as already explained, by successive experiences of "extra-ordinary" consciousness, experiences of a "larger Self" (the "observer plus Self-observer equals the witnessing-Self") as distinguished from the ordinary, "lesser self" (the engaged-in-activity-self). Temporarily, the two function separately.

A passage in which Strether may be seen noticing the phenomenon of separateness occurs when, entering a conversation with Mme. de Vionnet and Sarah, he is considering how much he can afford to give moral support to Mme. de Vionnet (faced as she is with Sarah's insinuations), and he stands by and ruminates a mo-

---

[4] I repeat the argument in James's essay here because of the importance it has as a link in the present discussion: consciousness, including the reception of sensory knowledge and the interpretation of it—the process of perception—occurs in the mind. James speaks of a process which he says "can only be described as the accumulation of the very treasure [source] of consciousness itself," and it is here that he begins to identify the "sources" with higher (extra-ordinary) consciousness: he says he apprehends, through this accumulation, other combinations than observation and experience, in the ordinary sense, have given him a pattern of (224). James says: "I won't say 'the world,' as we commonly refer to it, grows more attaching, but will say the universe increasingly does, and that this makes us present at the enormous multiplication of our possible relations with it" (221).

ment. In describing this moment James makes use of one of many references in his work to consciousness as a vessel:

> If Mme. de Vionnet, under Sarah's eyes, had pulled him into her boat, there was by this time no doubt whatever that he had remained in it and that what he had really been most conscious of for many hours together was the movement of the vessel itself. They were in it together this moment as they hadn't yet been . . . . (240; 9, I)

Just as from the vessel he watches the life in the vessel, so he begins to notice the vessel itself; just as he notices the activity in the vessel, so he notices the (other) Self that also sees the vessel (that Self is the extra-ordinary one and has been referred to by James as if it were an "outer ring" around ordinary consciousness).

Recall that Strether's surrender to Mme. de Vionnet has been a surrender to himself; that a surrender to her is actually a surrender to his own transcendental awareness. On the one hand he now possesses an awareness of his individual existence with its individual wants and needs, while on the other he possesses an awareness of the transcendental Self.

The result of the separation is twofold. The new Self begins to function more closely with the old, reflecting on every object, activity or thought the hero encounters in that other, ordinary, active state. The distinction of Self and object disappears as more and more the two coordinate with each other. The person's sense of relationships and proportions, and his sense of wholeness and interconnectedness, expands. A passage that unmistakably demonstrates these qualities in Strether is his response to Sara's attack in Book 10 quoted earlier in Chapter I:

> Everything has come as a sort of indistinguishable part of everything else. Your coming out belonged closely to my having come before you, and my having come was a result of our general state of mind. Our general state of mind had proceeded, on its side, from our queer ignorance, our queer misconceptions and confusions—from which, since then, an inexorable tide of light seems to have floated us into our perhaps still queerer knowledge [queerer to *her*, the novice, that is]. (293; 10, III)

In addition to what he says literally, many things are implied here. To Strether, all things are interconnected; "my" actions are related to "yours" in a cause-effect chain. Out of past ("queer") ignorance came knowledge, light. That light had an inexorable tide, a fate controlling it, a force of nature. Our (my) actions synchronize with nature with such infinitely correlated intelligence that they seem to "go by themselves," but at the same time the movement caused by fate is easy and natural, if not enjoyable. (For *how* enjoyable see 297–99; II, I.)

The *Bhagavad-Gita* Commentary makes several statements that provide a highly appropriate comment on the state of consciousness Strether reveals in the passage just quoted (Brahman, a term used here, is the state of consciousness which realizes oneness of existence in all the diversity of action):

> All actions form an integral part of Brahman conscious-
> ness; *everything* is appreciated as none other than that conscious-
> ness . . . .
>
> The enlightened man is established in Brahman conscious-
> ness irrespective of the engagement of the mind and senses in
> action; he is intent on Brahman, while at the same time every-
> thing that action entails proceeds naturally at the level of the
> senses . . . .
>
> Ever established in that state . . . he is simply a silent witness
> of what is happening through time; he is a means by which nature
> fulfills its purpose of evolution . . . . (291)

In the second balcony scene, we see Strether's old and new consciousness coming together, the new coming together not just with the consciousness he had had long before in Woollett, but also the consciousness he had as late as his arrival in Paris and on to the present.

Just prior to the scene he makes the announcement mentioned before that he is "in possession as he never had been" (297; 11, I). The description he gives could be said to become, in concrete terms, a "definition" of the great change in his life that summer:

> He felt, strangely, as sad as if he had come for some wrong,
> and yet as excited as if he had come for some freedom. But the
> freedom was what was most in the place and the hour. It was the
> freedom that brought him around again to the youth he had long
> ago missed. He could have explained little enough today either
> why he had missed it or why, after years and years, he should care
> that he had; the main truth of the actual appeal of everything
> was nonetheless that everything represented the substance of his
> loss, put it within reach, within touch, to make it, to a degree it
> had never been, an affair of the senses. That was what it became
> for him this singular time, the youth he had long ago missed—a

queer concrete presence, full of mystery yet full of reality, which he could handle, taste, smell, the deep breathing of which he could positively hear. (298)

He begins here by describing an apparently contradictory state of mind: sadness *and* excitement. The double state is, for Strether at this singular time, "the youth he had long ago missed," but also, now, "*within reach*" . . . to an extent "*it had never been*" (297). It is full of mystery, yet full of reality—*immediate* reality, the reality of the senses, which "he could handle, taste, smell, the deep breathing of which he could positively hear." It is also part of a whole new world previously never dreamt of in his philosophy: "It was in the long watch from the balcony, in the summer night, of the wide late life of Paris . . . "(298).

Whatever he may also see in the past, the substance of this immediacy is seen from his new position, from his "Paris" consciousness. What he is saying is not simply that he feels nostalgic about his lost youth; he is saying it is in this life, this immediate Parisian one, that he is experiencing, tasting, the greatest reality.

He is able to spell out for us two important "products" of his experience: (1) "Freedom was . . . most in the place and the hour";[5] (2) "everything represented the substance of his loss." *How* he is free is a subject for detailed attention in the next Chapter. But he says he is free. What is his freedom? He has gained the freedom he speaks of through transcendence, that is, noninvolvement, the ability of the mind to witness or watch life no matter how one is involved. As to his loss, the objects and people and experiences of his youth before him in his memory, as if in panoramic vision, only partly represent his loss. That is, what the loss *was* is only part of the experience, because that loss is being transformed, and right now he is reseeing the substance of it. The old order is passing out of view (hence his sadness), and as it does so he sees the new order through the vision of Paris and all it stands for (hence his excitement). It is an apparent loss, really amounting to the giving up of certain kinds of perception and the establishment of a perception in another

---

[5] Strether, in one of his meditations prior to the last scene with Mme. de Vionnet, is struck by how "unpunitive" he feels in spite of her recent deception. Traditionally, he says, the "state of the wrongdoer" would present some difficulty. He is not in such difficulty at present. In fact, he is struck by "the ease of it—for nothing in truth appeared easier. It was an ease he himself fairly tasted of for the rest of the day; giving himself quite up, not so much as trying to dress it out, in any particular whatever, as a difficulty . . . (334).

form within the compass of the wide late life of Paris. Included in that compass is not only this re-electrification of the senses, but a widening of the camera lens that picks up the impulses. When both the keenness of the senses and the widening increase enough, when "perfect" alertness and "total" scope fully combine, he will identify with every object or idea or sense or sound in nature. (This type of growth, "the enlightened state," is more fully explained by a passage quoted from the *Gita* on the following page.)

The new vision in this passage, as we found elsewhere, is shifting from the old "subject-object" dualistic approach to one by which he sees the object as part of his own greater Self. He is dispensing with the "I" vs. "you," "we" vs. "they," and the "in here" vs. "out there" epistemology. He is finding, as a natural consequence, that the separation of observer and observed becomes less distinct as he identifies more and more with the objects of his perception. The more he identifies with *all* objects in reality, the more he knows the entire cosmos spontaneously in its entirety; the connecting substance is pure Being, or pure consciousness.

To summarize: To the two factors I called most important in this passage, loss and freedom, let us add a third: sense experience. The change Strether undergoes involves the first two factors in conjunction with the third; as he looks at, or resees, impressions of his youth, his sense of loss diminishes. As a result, he says he no longer misses his youth, and in fact he does not know why he ever did. What he feels instead is not just a new keenness of taste and touch and smell (with respect to youth) but a new keenness with respect to everything in his present life as well—he sees the concreteness, the fullness, and the mystery of reality.

This kind of renunciation is a result of transcendence. Recall the descriptions of Strether's transcending in previous chapters. It is clear that one cannot try to transcend. It happens. In the same way one does not try to "renounce." It happens. Thus the *Bhagavad-Gita* Commentary says:

> The principle of renunciation is only to be understood: it is
> not to be practiced . . . . Knowledge, or renunciation, is extolled
> here, not the practice of it . . . . Renunciation as such is plainly
> a state of loss [in the novel Strether's youthful manner of seeing
> succumbs to his new way of seeing this new consciousness]: it is
> union through loss. Renunciation here is to save life, not to lose
> it; it brings fulfillment to life. (326–27)

In another passage, which I quote here in connection with the same speech of Strether's, the *Gita* gives a description that is almost identical with his experience:

> When the enlightened state has been gained, the mind automatically functions from a level of its full potentiality, and the senses, having reached their full development, function at their highest capacity.
>
> The objects of the senses, however, remain unchanged. Thus the mind, acting from that level, experiences objects more completely, resulting in an ever greater appreciation of the object and thus providing experiences of greater happiness on the sensory level. The objects of sense are enjoyed more thoroughly than before, but because Being is more fully grounded in the very nature of the mind, the impression of sensory experience fails to capture the mind [fails to the extent that one sensory experience, though making a distinct impression, does not eclipse others and distort one's vision] . . . .
>
> The enlightened man thus naturally remains in a state where the senses continue to experience their objects while he remains free.[6] (343)

Thus the new sensory perception and new freedom relate to "loss": "loss" of Strether's "old geography" and his mode of perception. It affects his entire consciousness and is not the first such experience for him. A similar one occurs in a late afternoon conversation with Maria Gostrey after Strether's last visit with Sarah. Here he profits from awareness, but it is more significant that he hints at a connection between the loss-redemption syndrome and the growth of his "oneness of awareness." The subject of the conversation is Chad. Strether tells Maria:

S: I told her [Marie] I'd take it all [i.e., take the blame, the consequences, for what might happen].
M: You'd 'take' it?
S: Why if he doesn't go [back to Woollett].
M: And who takes it if he does? she enquired with a certain grimness of gaity.
S: Well, I think I take, in any event, everything.

---

[6] If he is enlightened, the changes in Strether would not be the result of personal intellectual choices; they would be based on physiological changes in the nervous system that result from repeated exposure to transcendence. The changes would permeate emotions, intellect, indeed, every function of his mind and body. They go far deeper than ratiocination.

M: By which I suppose you mean . . . you now lose everything. (311; 11, II)

He "takes" the entire blame of the world, or of his immediate world; he "takes" the loss resulting from his action in Paris, which in turn involves a great part of his previous years. Taking such blame is a form of identifying with, and sympathizing with, all things and all people, as well as losing "everything" (for Strether, that would include Mrs. Newsome, her money, the good will of the entire Newsome-Pocock clan, the respect of certain other citizens of Woollett, his job, and probably his reputation as an editor). He loses the "Woollett" kind of life (with its accompanying limitations); simultaneously he gains the "Paris" kind of life that for him means that oneness of awareness mentioned before. Loss through renunciation of the surrendering kind ends with subsequent gain; or renunciation, redefined here, becomes simultaneous loss and redemption; what is lost has become transformed into a new awareness.

As to his refusal to marry Maria, a number of Strether's new qualities should be considered: his "oneness of vision," his ability to turn loss into gain, his ability to live in the "now," his increased objectivity (wherein one part of his consciousness does not eclipse others), his noninvolvement, his equanimity or unchangeability, and his ability to experience not merely the parts of things that are in "active" or "nonlatent" consciousness but those not, at every moment, fully active in him.

All these qualities are part of the "new order" of Strether's life, and they afford us sufficient means of appraising his decision about Maria. James says in his "Project of Novel": "Marrying Gostrey would be of the old order" (Abridged 390); that goes to the heart of the matter.[7]

By now it is plain what James means by the "old order": it is "Woollett" and all it stands for. The new order, the "Paris" order, is more difficult to delineate and define. Strether might have thought, at the first full experiencing of it, that his discovery, his new consciousness, would be "spoiled" if he married (it would not). He might even have thought that he would be forced to give up his new-found identity. One could see how with this misconception he would think it imprudent to marry. We can allow him this; as a

---

[7] The statement does not mean that Gostrey is of the old order, but that marrying her would be so to him.

journeyman who has stumbled onto the universe of transcendence, he is a novice with no clear common guide as to its scope.

The primary characteristic of the new state of consciousness is "oneness of vision." Thus if Strether is intimately identified with all of human nature, in fact, all of *nature*, it must be clear to him (if not to others) that he is most useful and valuable as a single man, knowing and appreciating all things and people, yet not affixed to any one of them, an attachment which would make his general association to that extent exclusive. By the same token, from his larger knowledge, he would see himself as more valuable to both Maria and Marie as he is, not married to either one of them. He openly claims, in conversation with Maria, that something like this is true: "That's the way that—if I must go—you yourself would be the first to want me. And I can't do anything else" (365; 12, V).

The remarks in this final conversation do not, in isolation, say very much, but taken together they say a great deal. For instance, consider his remark that to be "right" he must not "get anything for himself" (365). In a negative sense, "to be right" simply means not to profit from all Maria has to offer.[8] This would be a denial, a *renunciation* in the old sense, of something in himself, of those naughty material profits. But if *that* is his motive, he is right back in Woollett, being good by being repressed. When one takes into account the new order, to be right must mean something more. At last Maria moves the focus away from that particular center by saying, "It isn't so much your being 'right'—it's your horrible sharp eye for what makes you so." So in the end, it all comes down to perception after all: it is the inner quality of his heart and mind that makes him internally 'right' and, in turn, externally right as well. What is *in* his perception, that is, the nature of his perception, and its change to a different one, has been described in this chapter. It results in his doing what he does for and through all things. And he acts through a consciousness rooted in internal and external order, in fluctuation and stability. It is a state of balance. "Right"-ness, then, is a faculty in the mind that balances or regulates opposing capabilities, as if the mind were a ship containing a gyroscope.

If he were to marry either of the two women, Mme. de Vionnet would be the logical choice, first because, though he is attracted

---

[8] Hers is an offer of "excellent service," he says, "of lightened care, for the rest of his days . . . . It built him softly round, it roofed him warmly over, it rested, all so firm, on selection. And what ruled selection was beauty and knowledge" (365).

to them both, he and Marie have that transcendent consciousness in common and could synchronize with each other in the deepest sense; and in such a combination they would more readily benefit the world around them. Of course, he cannot marry Marie because she is married. Perhaps, presuming she could fall out of love with Chad, he could have an affair with her. She reveals in their last scene together what he means to her as a friend, and now that he has grown so fond of her, readers can imagine Strether dreamily waiting around in Paris; in time, as she gets over Chad the two of them could drift away down the Seine.[9] He doesn't do or even try that.

The answer to numerous combinations one can devise for Strether's future is now always the same. Strether is a man who has found something so alluring, so wonderfully attractive to him, so utterly fulfilling that it supplants all other opportunities. "He has come through so far as to come out on the other side," Henry James says in The Notebooks (415). He knows the joy of something within him that cannot be described, it can perhaps be somewhat approximated with imagery—it is the joy of the silent moment he felt after his first conversation with Marie in Gloriani's garden, when he saw an intense light enveloping everything and at the same time in his mind he had a vision of the whole of life—what it meant and what one must do about it—all of which he tried to communicate to little Bilham in a speech at that moment. The expression— feeling—vision he had is something he now carries within himself everywhere. Having the means, not in terms of vision, but in terms of the activity that accompanies the vision, to do what his speech said one *should* do, he can live "all he can," or, to his fullest potential. He can do so because his immediate perception sees so well it sees all things within any given detail. The insight is so full it sees all implications of the immediate situation in proportion to the whole.

He does not *work* to keep the balance just described, it is simply there. And since it is, his occupation is one that he follows with great happiness. He is free to roam anywhere and everywhere with a response to his new perspective on the world that is ultimately satisfying because of the immense understanding of his approach.

---

9 "Madame de Vionnet had wished him to stay—so why didn't that happily fit? He could enshrine himself for the rest of his days in his young host's chambre d'ami and draw out these days at his young host's expense [Chad's that is]" (354; 12, IV).

Where others can enjoy the rewards of immediate physical gratifi-
cation and family life or some equivalent, they may not have his
capacity of vision and equanimity. But in his case it is not that
he "gives up" what they have. The joy and satisfaction of what he
experiences is so great that he feels no need to change.

Strether has made a tremendous discovery, that he has a Self,
and that it is of a most unusual kind. Early in the story he speaks of
his whole Paris experience as the "precipitation of his fate" which
bound him "in the direction of everyone and everything" (78; 1,
III). A similar notion is described in the *Gita*:

> When integration takes place, the person keeps his indi-
> viduality, but the glory of the inner Self . . . is infused into his
> feeling, his thinking, his vision, his whole field of experience . . . .
> [In this state] his vision is such that it quite naturally holds alike
> all things in likeness of his own Self, because he himself and the
> vision that he has are the expression of his own Self.[10] (448)

---

[10] "This [likeness of all things] does not mean that such a person fails to see a
cow or is unable to distinguish it from a dog. Certainly he sees a cow as a cow
and a dog as a dog, but the form of the cow and the form of the dog fail to
blind him to the oneness of the Self, which is the same in both. Although
he sees a cow and a dog, his Self is established in the Being of the cow and
the Being of the dog, which is his own Being . . . . The enlightened person
does not fall from his steadfast Unity of life, though acting in the whole of
diverse creation. That unity remains indelibly infused in his vision and he has
evenness of vision everywhere." (*Bhagavad-Gita* 359–60).

FREE WILL AND NECESSITY

I have pointed out that the process of transcendence gives Strether a feeling of inevitability; it does so at certain precise moments, but in addition, the entire experience of the summer has an inevitability about it for him. Strether is moving at this time in his life more and more rapidly toward his fate. The critical juncture in that movement is his seeing the young lovers in a boat in the country and deducing that they have spent the night together. Not only does he then discover their lie, but also he feels most deeply this inevitability along with a sense of wonder (of all things!)—and yet a sense of reality.

When he reviews the scene, Strether finds it all a "wonderful accident" (326; 11, IV), and as his recollection closes, he finds himself supposing "innumerable and wonderful things" (331). And in the middle of describing the events he says the facts were, "so far as one had to do with them, intrinsically *beautiful*." The wonderfulness, including the beauty, is most deeply revealed in the scene by the experience and the knowledge of intimacy Strether gains. Besides the lies, besides all the "fables" and "performances," which he sees with perfect clarity, Strether gradually works his way to the other side of the coin of the meaning of it all. Besides the "make-believe" factor that disagrees with his "spiritual stomach," there is the other feature of the show: the deep, deep truth of the intimacy revealed; or put in another way, the "deep, deep truth" passage, usually taken as a reiteration of the "make believe" that upsets his "spiritual stomach," is in fact an expression of the other feature, the truth, the reality of intimacy. Let me explain:

The scene is a little journey from appearances (lies) to reality. It happens just a second after he perceives Marie and Chad first catching sight of him. He sees them quickly decide how to play it: "They must have communicated all in silence. It was part of the deep impression for Strether, not the least of deep interest, that they could so communicate—that Chad in particular could let her know he left it to her . . . it in fact came over our friend in these meditations that there had been as yet no [better] illustration of his [Chad's] famous knowing how to live [than this one]" (330)

Here is an example of Strether's often-noted "opening his mind to the value of sense experience." He places his greatest appreciation not on the couple's illegitimacy, the make-believe he cannot stomach, but on their silent intimacy, that is, their silent understanding that is so intimate at the moment. It is as if the intimacy he discovers here has started to war with the ugliness he thought to find at the heart of illicit affairs. He is not merely, in other words, beginning to recognize that total intimacy is there, but he is beginning to see a form of knowledge enter that is new; intimacy, unmarried intimacy, can be something more than ugliness.

Marie's little act was a "performance" (329), a performance "destined to deepen" (328), to take him, as destined, from unreality to reality. The lie had seemed real; it had been "inevitably" in the air, something on which one could now, "detached and deliberate, perfectly put one's finger" (329); it is something they had eaten and drunk and talked and laughed over "during dinner and afterwards" (329). But then as we follow him, he points us in a new direction. He implies there are two sides: the false position and the (later) true one, the predicament at the beginning and the resolution of the whole connundrum at the end. When he was in the false position, his ordinary mind would have siezed upon the lie as treacherous. His new mind does not. The "real experience," he says, put on "what is most to our purpose" and that becomes "very wonderful indeed, wonderful for readiness, for beautiful assurance, and (especially) for the way her decision was taken on the spot" (329), because, he says, that decision resulted from something "communicated all in silence" (330) between the two, which fascinated him.

By implying that his mind took a new position, he is not saying he completely relinquished the old one (Mme. de Vionnet did lie to him). He is saying the mind contains steps; one experiences unreality, then reality; fiction or fable, then truth (the falsehood: all illicit affairs are ugly; the truth: some illicit affairs can be beautiful). Both steps are present as his attention moves from one to the other. Both are stages that portray a particular growth in himself. In the early days, before Gloriani's, he was "ill-directed." After Gloriani's, he experienced a new kind of motion; he was "well-directed." And how, after Gloriani's, he no longer moves simply by "ordinary" choice. The movement is "inevitable," or necessary, because in transcending, one's mind supercedes the flow of ordinary consciousness and allows itself to be directed by a larger, more completely natural, more completely spontaneous faculty of consciousness.

His mind goes through a "revolution" and comes out beyond it, "on the other side," "whole." It goes through the experience of the lie and comes out beyond it, trusting, then knowing (that is, the knowing is of a principle, not just a fact, and the principle grows out of having a wider mental perspective). On an individual, momentary basis, as in the teaching scenes with Marie, each experience has gone—inevitably for Strether—from activity to silence, from confusion to order, and from predicament to resolution. But also, on the basis of the *whole* Paris experience, it has been a growing transformation from ordinary to transcendent vision involving his outlook on life. His "outlook," and his choices, which mark his growth to Second Level, result less and less from personal fears and prejudices and increasingly from his proximity to the forces of nature as these correlate in *him* as well as infinitely and increasingly throughout the cosmos. To the extent that the forces contain all of nature, they are controlled by "necessity"—"fate." He is really saying in this passage that what happened (once and then repeatedly after he had had that transcendent moment in Gloriani's garden) was as bound to happen as if a tidal wave had swept him up and tossed him wherever he is now (or directed the growth of his mind to whatever condition it achieved after his initial transcendence). He does not object that the tidal wave is compelling him, forcing him along; on the contrary, he keeps saying in this passage, being close, as he is, to the end of his journey in Paris, and discussing, as he is, the conclusion of his scientific scrutiny of the couple, and of their intimacy, how intrinsically *beautiful* (328), how *wonderful* (329, 331), and how utterly true things have become. "Intimacy," he tosses at us, "is *like* that" (331).

Shortly after the scene ends, Strether goes to visit Chad; he views Chad's balcony, this time from the balcony itself. He sees in Chad's attitude "something more than a return"; indeed, he sees clearly "a conscious surrender." Strether refers to his present pursuit of Chad as "taking up his life afresh . . . . It [the pursuit] was dragging him, at strange hours . . . . It was keeping him out of bed at the end of long hot days; *it was transforming beyond recognition the simple subtle, conveniently uniform thing that had anciently passed with him for a life of his own*" (353).

These were his thoughts. As to the other, more typical needs one might imagine such a man concerned with—loneliness, a need to love or be loved (sexually or not), a need to take more notice of Gostrey, Gostrey's need for a partner and companion, and a hundred such considerations—he does not mention one of them. His first thought is that he no longer has "a life of his own." At this point he has come back to the major dilemma he has been wrestling with all along—he finds himself selecting the life his changing perception has uncovered, weighing not just his own needs against other's but his former world against his new one. And then he says, "There was literally a minute—it was strange enough—during which he grasped the idea that as he *was* acting, as he could only act, he was inconsistent. The sign that the inward forces he had obeyed really hung together would be that—in default always of another career—he should promote the good cause by mounting guard on it" (354). When the forces really hung together, he would not just "understand" the good cause (in this case, the merits of intimacy, i.e., sexual intimacy, even when one of the persons is married), but promote and protect it. And he says he is virtually "dragged" along toward what he must do (in this case, about Chad). He must not, in short, live a life of his own. "Why should it concern him that Chad was to be fortified . . . [and] reaffirmed [and] reassured? There was no answer to such a question but that he was still practically committed—he had perhaps never yet so much known it." He knows he must follow whatever reality his new perception of the world unfolds.

All the time that "fate" or necessity appears to be encircling him only to force him somewhere, he is overcome, ironically, by a growing sense of freedom. In fact, because he delights so much in telling us how free he feels, the old saying that freedom is a state of mind (that is, a condition of mind, one that is real, and by *no* means an illusion) seems quite appropriate. And does the other typical notion, that with freedom one can "go or do as one pleases," apply as well? Strether's freedom starts in his ability to step back and see the world from another world or another perspective (described in Chapter V of this book); he learns to take himself away from a "Woollett" mind and realize a "Paris" one and reflect on both. Ultimately, in the sense that it cradles the thoughts that he now lives by, the Paris mind *is* freedom because it represents a type of thought indigenous to the enlightened person; the essential part of freedom, the core of it, is "pure" thought, pure "thatness," or pure consciousness—these being the stuff of the larger Self. The essential part of pure consciousness is noninvolvement, whose real meaning is *involved* noninvolvement. As noninvolved, or free, his Self affords Strether certain capacities: independence, equanimity (which one could translate in his present circumstances as even-handedness), freedom from possessiveness, and freedom from prejudice and fear. What *causes* this last condition is that the self is now identified with all things and all people, oneness with the whole of nature; transcendence of the kind Strether has known infuses the mind with, or opens it up to, this capacity for all-inclusiveness (Chapter VI, pp. 116, 119 and 121).

As to Strethers' happiness: were he given the choice to live his whole life over again, would Strether not choose the Parisian experience? And would he not even ask that everything be very close to what he has just been through? After all, he is experiencing the greatest happiness he has ever known. Since that happiness is based on the transcendental order of his mind, he must have discovered it, for whatever reason, where he now is, on the Second Level, as a "state of mind" or as a condition of consciousness—not an illusion—not a mind with consciousness pounded into a "tin mould." It had been that to him once—no longer. He once thought freedom was an illusion because he had not experienced any appreciable degree of real freedom. Earlier, when he saw it as an illusion, he had experienced the burden of life's responsibilities without the buoyancy of transcendence, without the certainty of being part of everything (138; 5, II).

Now, responsibilities (i.e., necessities) are met *in accordance with* free choices that, in turn, consistently lead to greater happiness. He would now see that happiness must have been his destiny, as he looked back in life, not only in the time frame of this novel, but also in terms of his life before that. On the strength of his present achievement, his mind would start to resee and reshape his vision of those events. In view of what happened, he might see all of his past as a conditioning process for receiving his present awareness and happiness. That awareness would start with his first glimpse, somewhere in the past, of transcendental consciousness (unknown to him then in his ordinary consciousness), enough to enliven the potential awareness already present in his mind.

As to Strether's freedom, had we asked him before this summer and before he found his "Second Level" if he had been free earlier in life, he might have thought this was absurd. But more and more, as he grew into the Second Level and noticed the appearance of the new freedom, he would see that the possibility of it had always been there in his mind, potential, dormant, waiting to be discovered. He would then say that his early life had been without freedom, but only to the extent that he did not know what freedom was.

His discovery parallels what Einstein's experiment (described in Chapter II, p. 38) says about perception of the physical world: what each person sees in time and space is relative to his own situation; or, as in Strether's case, his own level of consciousness.

Up to this point in the novel, necessity (the inevitability of things) and freedom would appear to be independent experiences in Strether's mind; but now the two seem to be converging and becoming parallel elements in his spiritual and mental constitution. But is this possible? Can we have a case of free will and necessity functioning in combination?

An answer is offered by Anthony Campbell, an English physician and teacher of meditation who made a thorough study of the nature of meditation and enlightenment in his TM and the Nature of Enlightenment:

> On the conceptual level, to say that we are free although our actions are determined by the ebb and flow of cosmic forces is a contradiction; if we try to understand this intellectually, we inevitably take hold of one horn of the dilemma to the exclusion of the other, and the natural result is either complete irresponsibility or complete submission to "fate." It is vital to understand that the true state of liberation, although it can be described, cannot be imagined; it can only be lived. For most of us, the nearest we come to it is at moments of artistic or intellectual creation, when everything is seen to be both right and inevitable. J. S. Bach said, "I play the notes in order, as they were written. It is God who makes the music." That state of liberation, it appears,

is one in which we (freely) perform our actions in order, as they
were written. (203)

There are some who think this combination of free will and
necessity is a real possibility in life. But let us set aside for the
moment the question of whether it is possible in life (by which I
mean "real life," as we say, as distinct from fiction) and address the
question of its appearance in fiction. Two features of fiction seem
to me to make such a combination more easily accomplished than
it would be in real life. The first is that everything in a work of
fiction is, if not controlled, then at least *conceived* by one author, so
that what becomes a sphere of influence anywhere in the story can
be said to have originated somewhere in the author as the god of a
fictional universe who sometimes, with remarkable skill, can make
the forces of necessity coincide with free will. Henry James has done
so in *The Ambassadors*. The second feature is peculiar to the work of
James, and most especially to *The Ambassadors*; it is the possibility
of a form of interaction, or communication, not supernatural, not
verbal, and certainly not noticeable to everyone in the story—
something like a pressure exerted subliminally on the creative world
of the characters. I am referring to what appears to be a wave, or
a force field; and, depending on the needs of the author's time-
period and his total artistic conception, this force, or these forces,
seem to have an influence fundamental enough to affect, in fact to
effect the basic thinking patterns of characters. Indeed, they alter
the climate of thought of the community at large.[1] As I said, the
"wave" would be something which functions more deeply than the
level of speech (though it functions on that level as well). One can
see that Marie de Vionnet's consciousness, on an individual basis,
has an unusually powerful effect on the consciousness of Strether.
It is as if some form of energy outside the ordinary conventions of
the drama were operating that we could easily miss or perhaps have
missed in the past. But was the influence on Strether exerted only
through the Countess's words, her manner of dress, her looks and

---

[1] Sociological research has shown that the field of consciousness can produce
"action at a distance" as well as other field-like phenomena. In studies of groups
practicing together the Transcendental Meditation and TM-Sidhi program (a
more advanced technique), researchers have found that just as the application
of a magnet at one location affects the entire electromagnetic field, so these
meditating groups can improve the brain wave coherence and the behavior of
other groups of individuals at a distance. There are over twenty-five different
studies documenting this group dynamics of consciousness. Notable among
them are two published by David W. Orme-Johnson and colleagues.

gestures, and those thoughts which precede and follow her words, or was it something less tangible, ultimately more effective than any of these—a kind of attraction/repulsion system that is as swift and penetrating as a laser beam?

In both scenes in which Gloriani appears, one a gathering at his own home and another at Chad's, he practically never speaks out loud, yet his influence is like an invisible beam that throws itself everywhere, not just on Chad and his friends, but on the other artists, other friends, and persons he does not even know. In their first meeting in his garden, Gloriani's effect seemed to Strether personal and deliberate (the "god" had spoken). The "quality" says the author, had "appeared . . . to turn him [Strether] inside out" (163, 6, II). In the second visit, even though that personal link between the two was gone, the influence was still everywhere; and now Strether watches the artist

> paying the place . . . by the manner of his presence and by something Strether fancied he could make out in this particular glance, such a tribute as, to the latter's sense, settled many things once for all. Strether was conscious at this instant, for that matter, as he hadn't yet been, of how, round about him, quite without him, they *were* consistently settled. (162)

Depending on the meaning of the sweeping phrase "many things," Strether's musings could be gently touching upon a tremendous arsenal of power somewhere. The presence of the man (Gloriani) himself has the power to "settle" the disorders, the confusion, in something like the molecular structure of the atmosphere and in the minds of all around—and for how far? His influence could be endless. It is as if, not just the isolated minds of different individuals present, but the area around the minds, and the parts of those minds that enable them to make contact in some deeper form of consciousenss are affected—it is as if all these things in the environment had previously been "unsettled," but with one moment of his attention everything has been transformed. Singly, Gloriani's presence certainly affected Strether himself and then affected the group Strether had met through Chad; but his effect on the city in general (though subterranean) from the treatment the author has given him, from his mystical proportions, might have been overwhelming. One can imagine that a fullness had elected to replenish an emptiness or a lack of some kind in the "collective unconscious." Perhaps its source could be a positive electric field that his presence activated, that has been introduced to counter-balance a competing negative field. An example can be found in *The Ambassadors* in the river scene when we watch the silent communication of Marie and Chad in the boat in combination with the recognition Strether has from the shore, not just his recognition of who they were, but of the power of what he was seeing and learning at the same moment. Another example of the activity of "force-fields" similar to one already given but this time producing an immediate change, is the way in which a character, in the middle of a conversation communicates on a subliminal plane so much more keenly than the conversation itself reveals. (This feature of *The Ambassadors* is also to be found elsewhere in Henry James's fiction, but *especially* in the late novels.) In a passage I quoted earlier (Chapter III), Strether comments on his conversation with Mme. de Vionnet, who has suddenly made a deep impression on him:

> At the back of his head, behind everything, was the sense that she was—there, before him, close to him, in vivid imperative form—one of the rare women he had so often heard of, read of, thought of, but never met, whose very presence, look, voice, the mere contemporaneous *fact* of whom, from the moment it was at all presented, made a relation of mere recognition. (156; 6, I)

Finally, Strether himself has an opportunity to initiate an energy of this kind that is as strong as his model's. In the end, in the manner of Isabel returning to Gilbert and Rome, Strether returns to Woollett. And there will be a great need for his presence, because *his* positive electrical force, or his fullness, will indeed encounter a negative or an empty one: the Pococks, the Newsomes and the rest of the clans of his old days will be, not the negative field itself, but the signal of it. Let us assume that he does carry out his promise to go to Woollett. The reason Strether would immediately recognize this characterization of his next move is that his evolution from the initial moment in the garden of Gloriani has been precisely toward such a counterbalancing role. Since his consciousness has moved by degrees into synchrony with the forces of nature, the answer to one of the most frequently asked questions about Strether, "where will he go after Paris?" is simply: He will go where he must—and he will want to. And because he knows this, his growth, as we have seen it, is toward a response that combines all the forces of nature, so his freedom grows too as he realizes the total significance of it, watches each moment unfold, and knows he is moving by free choice toward fulfillment.

Let me point out one more facet of this theory that makes it appropriate for fiction, at least for Henry James's fiction, if not, indeed, for fiction in general; an author working singly can treat his fictional world as an organic whole, in which case these organic undercurrents can be made believable. If in "real life" a people in some part of the world should remain convinced that man, though an organic creature, is at war with a largely inorganic world of nature, which is equivalent to saying that nature is mechanical and rudderless, the system of force fields in that society would be a doomed proposition before it began. (For a more extended discussion of this concept of force fields as it relates to Strether's final choice and to how Strether can be said to relate to motion in nature, see the Appendix.)

Anthony Campbell takes a long look at the implications of such underlying fields in an attempt to see if they have historical reality. He says that for a long time Western man believed in a personal God who promulgated edicts to him, as would a law-giver governing his subjects by decree. This attitude had a far-reaching effect on the development of modern science. "Thinkers of the nineteenth century quite naturally pictured the universe as a giant mechanism constructed and set going by the Great Artificer. And when the notion of a personal God finally disappeared from science altogether, all that was left was a soulless mechanism operating according to impersonal laws." In contrast, in the East, especially in the cases of both China and India, "the universe was regarded, not as being composed of dead matter wholly separate from mind, but as an organic unity in which human life was one strand in an overall pattern." He continues, "We are now at the point [in the West] where we are being forced, by the logic of our own scientific discoveries toward a more organismic view of nature—a view which has much in common with that of the ancient Far East" (197).

To illustrate the possibility of an interaction of forces beneath the surface in nature, Campbell first mentions the phenomenon of simultaneous inventions that appear at different times in history—inventions such as toothed wheels, the water wheel, and the camera obscura that were made almost simultaneously in both Europe and China, although no direct cross-influence has ever been traced. Those scientists in the West with a rigidly materialistic view of human life, he says, have never made much headway in providing an answer for this simultaneity. But one exception to the stereotype is C. G. Jung, whose collective unconscious has a number of features similar to the subterranean forces in nature we have been describing above. Jung says:

> Each individual is like an island projecting above the surface of the sea, separate from all the others above the water line but joined with them below. At a superficial level, minds (and thoughts) are individual, but at a deeper level they are one. (Quoted by Campbell 194)

To Jung, not only is there an interplay of forces at the deeper level (laterally), but a hidden interchange is constantly going on between unconscious and conscious levels. Thus the psyche is to be explained ecologically; it is a result of the interplay of many factors seeking to come into balance. It follows that history and society do not result from cultural contacts alone, but also from this deeper interplay; thus the simultaneous appearance of similar ideas and discoveries throughout the world at certain times is the outcome of changes in the ecological system.

Another exception, though not Western, is to be found in the *Bhagavad-Gita*. In his Commentary on the *Gita* which I have been referring to in this text, Maharishi Mahesh Yogi explains that there are in nature three underlying forces the *Gita* calls "gunas" (128–29). One of these is a positive (creative) force and another is negative (destructive), while the third acts as an interceptive regulator of the other two. These forces strive to keep every aspect of life properly balanced with every other aspect, and the tension involved keeps nature moving in an evolutionary direction. But that balance, that equilibrium in nature, can be lost, whereupon instead of evolutionary balance, chaos and decay can result. When that balance is threatened, waves of positive energy and fullness—somewhat akin to what Lambert Strether experiences of a transcendent nature personally in his later life, or somewhat like the impetus of Gloriani on the community in which he lives—come into play to restore the evolutionary balance in nature and society as a whole.

Thus, according to the *Gita* as interpreted by Maharishi, the universe is not soulless and dead, but an organismic "creature," and human values emerge from and find their justification in the structure of that kind of cosmos. Within that structure are energy fields, not identical in Jung and the *Gita*, but having important similarities.

Now if we turn again to fiction, where a more simplified and controlled situation is possible, we can see how such forces

might be pictured in a concrete sense. Consider Strether as capable
of producing a positive field of influence such as we have been
describing. When the scene opens on the river bend, a preparation
and a growth, indeed a transformation, have occurred in his life; he
has a consciousness that would naturally react according to its new
and extraordinary composition in response to whatever confronts
him. Marie and Chad appear on the scene in a boat and on the
spot unwittingly reveal their present and past charade. Had Strether
not been equipped with his new mode of perception, had he merely
been the man from Woollett we met in his first conversation with
Maria Gostrey at Chester, the result might have been destructive,
if not disastrous. Not just because of the uncontrollable response
he would generate or the hurt feelings he could cause to others,
but because the positive understanding that arises in his conscious
would, being reversed, reverberate negatively throughout nature and
society. As it is, he responds as Strether responds to other potential
consequences of the events: first he discovers the lie, then his mind
in its infinitely positive capability, realizing there is more truth than
was ever dreamed of in the situation, converts what could have been
a disaster into a new understanding. And the consequences go on
and on in the "organismic" (to James—though he would not use
this word) universe in which Strether resides.

A plausible explanation for such a reversal, it seems to me,
is that the mind, in transcendence, is put into contact with the
basis of these larger forces of nature, not simply by experiencing
one or the other pole of the positive and negative forces but by
being immersed in a third element, a field from which positive and
negative forces ultimately spring and through which they become
unified.[2] That field would be something one reaches in transcending
the opposing forces as an individual, or in a more general way
through a transcendence that occurs in a larger segment of the
population, sometimes enough to set in motion major evolutionary
advances; but this time, in speaking of a field, I have in mind,
not just that ultimate level of consciousness, "pure consciousness"
alone, which I have sought to explain in these pages, but a field

---

[2] Other experiments indicate behavior change in addition to the consciousness
change of the previous experiments mentioned in the footnotes on page 54–55.
In medium-sized cities throughout the country meditation teachers monitored
FBI crime reports and hospital accident reports. Results shows that when the
number of persons learning the practice of TM in a city reaches one percent of
the population, the accident and crime rates drop an average of eight percent
per year (Dillbeck).

that many advanced physicists treat as if it were a computer chip layout at the basis of all the forces of nature, the unified field. If consciousness, through transcending, *can* enter and explore such a field, then when he transcends, man indeed has the potential to immerse his consciousness in that "layout," that "central panel" of all the laws of nature. In transcending, he breaks free from his individual self and discovers his larger one, almost as if in a dream one were to find himself free of the active events of his life, floating outside of them, watching.

Thus transcendence gives Strether his freedom, and transcendence-as-freedom guides him to his destiny; in doing so he would simultaneously be free at every step to back away from the connecting circuits that link him to the panel if he chose to do so. On the other hand, the long-term rewards of choosing to go in the direction the panel indicates would, increasingly, encourage him to continue in that direction (this effect would take place because of the nature of the panel—it unifies all of nature, that is, everything possible in life). To the extent that Strether has succeeded in making solid, continual contact with his "panel," he is enlightened. To the extent that he has not, he is not. The passages of *The Ambassadors* discussed earlier in this chapter, which describe both his movement toward destiny and his joy in the freedom of choice he has as he goes along, indicate that he is moving toward that enlightenment, that he may be close to it, and certainly that what he has accomplished thus far has affected his life in its entirety.[3]

---

[3] The Appendix goes more fully into the nature of the unified field and the repercussions of Strether's movement toward it.

APPENDIX

The Unified Field Theory of Physics and
The Question of Strether's Motivation

Though not the major part of this book, it is certainly interesting from the point of view of Strether's development to higher consciousness that a relatively new direction is taking place in modern physics that is applicable to the hero of *The Ambassadors*. Toward the end of Chapter VII, in mentioning a "panel" theory, I had in mind the unified field theory of physics, which states that the whole of nature, the infinitely expanding universe, is sustained within itself on the level of a unified field.

The point of the next few pages is to explore the possibility that Strether's experience of pure consciousness, or the Second Level of consciousness, is identical with the unified field of physics. If it is, the capacity of Strether's mind as enlightened can be even more deeply and extensively understood than I have suggested so far. It also means that such descriptions of Strether's consciousness as "one with all the laws of nature" (Chapter V) and the notion of human life (in life *or* fiction) having undercurrents of consciousness— "fields"—that affect the community at large, may have a more specific and definite meaning in terms of contemporary thought than has yet been acknowledged.

As a novice aspiring to gain further knowledge of the scientific part of the conception just mentioned, I consulted many people;

among them were two consciousness specialists: John C. Hagelin,[1] a renowned authority on unified field theory (UFT) who, in addition to offering the nontechnical picture of UFT which follows, makes further remarks about the connection of UFT with pure consciousness; and Jeffrey Ritter, an expert on consciousness in general, a teacher of meditation and master of advanced techniques whose scientific background includes more than a cursory interest in unified field theory. Ritter was so keen about the idea of a literary character he could watch become enlightened that he made a study of both *The Ambassadors* and this complete manuscript, *Henry James and the Evolution of Consciousness*, to prepare to comment, as I requested, on whatever aspect of the study he chose. The abbreviated remarks which follow can hardly be said to explain the intricate, difficult subject of UFT, but it might give a reader totally unfamiliar with the subject a starting point. For those who wish more information, Hagelin has permitted me to include some passages from his lectures. These follow the "Conversation with Ritter" (p. 146). Following that is the larger description of UFT from which the present one was taken.

HIGHLIGHTS OF HAGELIN'S EXPLANATION

The unified field approach is based on the principle that the surface diversity of nature emerges from an underlying unity. At the nuclear level of nature's functioning, four forces underlie all other forms in nature. Recently these forces have been shown to be combined in a unified field.

---

[1] John C. Hagelin is Professor of Physics and Director of the Doctoral Program in Physics at Maharishi International University. Dr. Hagelin received his B.A. Summa Cum Laude from Dartmouth College in 1975. After completing his Ph.D. at Harvard University in 1981, he joined the theoretical physics group at the European Laboratory for Particle Physics (CERN) and the Stanford Linear Accelerator Center (SLAC), where he became actively engaged in fundamental research at the forefront of supersymmetric unified field theories. Following his positions at CERN and SLAC, Dr. Hagelin joined the faculty of Maharishi International University, where he established a doctoral program in elementary particle physics and unified quantum field theories. To date he has published over thirty articles in physics journals on such topics as "What Does b^- Quark Decay Tell Us About CP Violation?" *Proceedings of the 2nd Moriond Workshop*, 1982 (New Flavours, Editions Frontieres, Gif-sur-Yvette, France); "Spin-Zero Leptons and the Anomalous Magnetic Moment of the Muon," *Phys. Lett.*, 116 B, 1982; "Supersymmetric Relics from the Big Bang," *Nucl. Phys.*, 1984, and "Perhaps Scalas Neutrinos are the Lightest Supersymmetric Partners," *Nucl. Phys.*, 1984.

In recent times, the term "elementary particle" has been used in connection with the most basic level of matter. But the term has been a misnomer. The so-called "elementary particles" are really just excitations of more abstract and fundamental entities called "quantum fields."

Quantum fields are lively at the surface level of life, but also function at the deeper levels as "heavy" quantum fields; these heavy quantum fields pervade everything, but on a subtle level. The goal of modern physics has been to find one such quantum field from which all others emerge; the final frontier of this program is to be found at a level called the Planck Scale (10^{-35} cm). This is the "point value" of physics, the smallest conceivable distance, because at that level the gravitational field becomes so intense that even the familiar structure of space-time dissolves. When physics transcends space-time, it becomes meaningless to speak of space and time, or any sort of distance at all.

Arising from the Planck Scale is a principle known as supersymmetry. It is through supersymmetry that physics has been able to explore the fine-scale structures of the quantum level and to unify the four underlying forms of nature. According to Hagelin, unification based on supersymmetry provides the basis for the emergence of an entirely new theoretical model, a single field which embodies the totality of all the laws of nature as inseparable components of a self-sufficient, infinitely dynamic field whose limitless creativity remains a constant reality. That reality can be located at every point in creation. This is the unified field.

One can experience the unified field through meditation, directly, as the least excited state of one's consciousness. The reason for this is as follows: on a theoretical level the intellect seemed at one time to be based very fundamentally on time, space, and causation, but with the quantum geometry of the unified field, there is no ability to distinguish past and future. Time diminishes or virtually disappears; and space manifests itself in such a way that to define distance in a classical sense seems impossible. Thus there is absolutely no place for the intellect to put its foot. It seems that it is not the domain of the intellect to function outside space and time, but rather of some structure of knowledge itself causally prior to space and time. In terms of the human mind, that structure of knowledge is to be found in transcendence, which takes the mind beyond space and time. In order to live the total potential of natural law, one must take the attention to the point value (i.e., transcendental or pure consciousness), the state of maximum alertness where consciousness is most dynamic and all the laws of nature are fully enlivened. This level of consciousness is also the level in physics (the unified field) from which nature itself must function for life to unfold all its possibilities.' (See p. 157 for fuller development of this section.)

*   *   *

The remarks that follow by Ritter on Strether's motivation first began to take shape when he and I tried an exploratory conversation about UFT and *The Ambassadors*, taping the discussion with the idea of composing a prose statement for this Appendix. Reviewing the tape, it seemed to me that, except for some minor editing, because of its own spontaneity and clarity, the conversation should be offered in full. The result is something both unorthodox and unusual. Ultimately the reader will have to judge the wisdom of such an approach; but one cannot help noticing how the conversation brings out some extraordinary possibilities for Lambert Strether's consciousness.

CONVERSATION WITH RITTER

JR: I think you might be able to make a case for an analogy between the unified field theory and the novel on two levels: the level of character and the level of location; that is, the first would use the characters Strether, Marie and Gloriani, and the second the locations of Woollett, Paris and Rome.

CJ: How do you mean?

JR: The Strether of "Woollett" is sound asleep; Gloriani is wide awake. In fact, in one set of dimensions you could say Gloriani is the Christ figure or the enlightened avatar or just "the one who is awake." And Marie de Vionnet is the one who is "in between." She is the channel between the other two. That's how the analogy works on the level of the characters. As you have shown, the same analogy works in another way on the level of the physical location of the characters, starting with Paris. Rome is the Eternal City, a metaphorical heaven. Gloriani left Rome "in the middle of his life" and came to Paris. Paris is the channel between Rome and Woollett; these two are the ends of a spectrum and as such don't receive much consideration. That is, the novel does not take place in Woollett or in Rome. They are both alluded to as the extreme ends of that spectrum as if they were the range of a field that's being talked about. Now, the field of which they are a part is analogous to the unified field in physics. The unified field is something like a universal soil from which everything in the universe ultimately springs. In unified field theory, the whole universe is a "self-referral state."

CJ: What is a "self-referral state?"

JR: Conceptually, we can think of the universe as relative, all relativities taken together. You could say that all values of everything that exist are different expressions of some underlying field. On that level, of an underlying field, all qualities in creation find their ultimate resolution, their ultimate basis; and from that basis, everything else arises—everything in the relative sphere of life: potential ideas, pure creativity, and the purest humanitarian vision of what a human being is and can become; and, we must bear in mind, so also arises all of the sensitivity to art and all of the religious tradition that flows from Rome as well as all of those other conceptions that are conjured up by the simple use of that word, "Rome." The other end of the spectrum is Woollett, Massachusetts, a newly industrialized town at the turn of the century during the industrial revolution, with smoke stacks belching gray smoke, child labor, misery and oppression—human welfare being trampled by the machinery of progress; the absolute opposite end of the spectrum of that humanitarian ideal that the term "Rome" engenders. The two extremes find a resolution in Paris. Here we find Gloriani the artist *molding in clay*. I found that attribute of Gloriani you alluded to most interesting. In the Bible, man is made of clay and he's molded by the hands of God into this creature that we call a human being. Gloriani uses clay to mold unmanifest, purely creative ideas into these beautiful works of art. That takes place in Paris, which is where the two worlds become enmeshed. Maybe "molded" is a better word than "enmeshed." Paris is where the two worlds get molded into a greater unity, into a transcendental reality. Woollett and Rome conflict with each other, because they're both necessary to provide the balance. That's why Paris is a fulcrum. It's also the reason why Strether does not feel compelled to stay in Paris, because going back to Woollett is really going back to here. He never really left Woollett. In a true sense he simply transcended Woollett. It was always there, it was always with him, it always will be with him. All he's done is to add an appreciation of Rome by transcending that early value and eventually bringing it (Rome) with him back to Woollett. This enhances the reality of Woollett considerably. If he'd stayed in Paris he might have become static, nondynamic. There wouldn't be the dialectic of motion that you do have as produced by this analogy of the trilogy of cities. What's very important is the motion (or nonmotion at times) of the character through time and space as he grows in consciousness. So motion is a very important construct in The Ambassadors. It is important because, in another sense, Strether doesn't move. At the beginning of the book one could say he's on his way to Rome, spiritually at least, and the spirit of the story transpires in Rome; and then he's leaving Rome to return to Woollett. But the fact is, there's only a tiny range of movement on the physical plane, if any; yet on the plane of consciousness there's tremendous motion, from Woollett all the way to Rome and all the way back to Woollett. Again, the actual physical movement expressed by the characters is an insignificant amount, but it contains in it a seed value of the range of motion of consciousness, in terms of ideas, of the whole universe.

CJ: Somehow I have the feeling that the unified field theory can also be tied in with the different intensities of light in the light imagery of James and the Einstein parallel I used in Chapter II, more so than I've already done.

JR: My understanding is this: Einstein's theory points out that the underlying constant is the speed of light. And as a constant, it could express the value of the creation, maintenance and destruction of energy. That's all light is, matter in motion, or at least for the moment let's consider it that way. Or, energy in motion (matter equals energy), matter being a kind of measuring tool for the motion of light. Sometimes seers and visionaries refer to light as if all physical matter were nothing but light frozen within boundaries, and in fact as if the universe were nothing but light. In that sense the essential constituent of matter would be light, or "energy"; the only thing changing would be the expression of light and, while the speed of it is constant, its expression in terms of time and space would be what varies and gives rise to all the diverse aspects of creation. Maybe that's what James is doing—giving rise to the underlying value of light in a variety of different ways.

CJ: Well, the underlying value of consciousness anyway. I'm not sure about the value of physical light. Let's make a distinction. Let's say there is a difference between the "seer" type and the "physicist" type of light. Seers, visionaries, poets and the like use the term "light" to signify knowledge, revelation, deep insight and that sort of thing. Some are just borrowing from the environment—from sunlight—to make an image that conveys the abstraction they want, such as knowledge. But many seers have an inner experience of light (recall R. M. Bucke's description quoted in Chapter III, p. 53). They see *within* what appears to be light; it is quite different from what one sees every day, but it is there; it is white and intense, and they *call* it light. Now you mentioned a possible equation of light and "the whole of creation" in a conversation with me before, but since you were just speculating, I contacted, in Dr. Hagelin's absence, his associate chairman, Dr. Ashley Deans, who said a physicist would not say "matter is nothing but light"—but a poet or seer might choose to see it that way and might even be right in another sense. Let me explain: according to Dr. Deans, for you to say "the essential constituent of matter is energy" is correct. (And matter *is* energy.) Now about light: to a physicist light is "an excitation of the electro-magnetic field"; true, that field is related to the unified field, but it is several levels apart from it.[2] So the term "light" may be a visible representation of the unified field but is not literally that field itself.

What they could be experiencing, Deans suggests, are "excitations of the unified field." Whether the visionary experience is actual light or not doesn't seem to matter as far as what we are saying here goes.[3] One could be experiencing, howsoever indirectly, contact with the unified field, the most basic element in creation.

---

[2] At finer time and distance scales the electromagnetic field becomes unified with the weak W and Z fields. At even finer time and distance scales, the electroweak and strong forces combine at the level of grand unification; and ultimately, at the Planck scale, gravity is also unified, leaving just the "unified field" (Dr. Ashley Deans in a letter to Courtney Johnson, April 18, 1986).

[3] Perhaps more important than the light is the feeling or ("ineffable") experience accompanying the light. Meditators interviewed sometimes call the feeling, which is both a mental and bodily experience, omniscience or bliss or love. See the extensive descriptions in Chapter III.

JR: Yes, it may be true that this light is not directly identifiable with the unified field on a physical basis. But the term "light" still communicates the idea of the unified field perfectly. Recall the two levels of light in the garden passage at Gloriani's. Now think of physical light. Physical light can be two things: it can be a particle or a wave; it expresses properties. When it is giving expression to its "particle" nature, it is called a "photon," and we can measure photons of light. In a certain physical experiment you hold a very sensitive instrument up to, say, a lamp like this one, and the light coming from the lamp causes light pressure on the instrument— the equivalent of little particles bombarding the instrument to measure a pressure just like atmospheric pressure or any other kind of pressure. If it is true that on that level light is the expression of a flow of energy which causes a pressure to be measured—maybe a wave pressure or a "particle" pressure—you can see why one might think of all physical matter as one form of light. And what you say of enlightened people may also be true—they see creation as light—the embodiment of light—in all its relative aspects; but also, to them, objects, people, thoughts, ideas—all things that exist— appear to be manifestations of an *underlying* "light." So for the "seers" we have two different forms of light, the surface and the underlying light. The thing that connects everything together is this underlying light, in physicists' terms, the unified field. That could be precisely what James is driving at in his use of the analogy of light (remember, in the garden passage, there is "ordinary" light, the light of everyday life, the light of the "non-transcending" mind, and "extra-ordinary" light, the light of extra-ordinary experiences, the light of transcendence. The one is to the other as a 40-watt bulb is to a laser beam). Where the *motion in the novel stops*—where the characters are not moving forward, where the plot (activity of thought) "slows down"—there's an opportunity for the more intense light underlying everything else, suddenly to be "seen." This light is there all the time, but it's only seen when the characters slow down—in the garden, or the French countryside, or again in Marie's drawing room late in the book: and every time light is depicted, there is calm, giving the opportunity for that light of the unified field to be seen. It has always been there, but the reader can see it only when given the opportunity to do so. And transcendence works just that way. We see the pure light of creation when we are calm enough to see it—to listen to it. When we are established in "being" strongly enough, we can perform action (in the less intense light of day) without losing sight of the light of being.

Let me drop back a minute to the "motion" of the characters once more. The idea of the characters coming to know themselves while moving from "here to here," of going nowhere except in their own minds—of moving "in their selves," so to speak. That notion or conception is most obvious in Strether, because he has the farthest distance to travel to get to know himself. But even in the other characters—in Chad Newsome and Madame de Vionnet—we see change; we see growth during the course of the novel. They're still coming to know themselves. It's a more relative kind of change vis-a-vis the "absolute" change Strether is going through, and perhaps this is so for the very reason that light comes first where it is darkest. The light has to come up and start speaking, absorbing that first ray of sunshine when it comes, and it takes a more intense light and even a relatively brighter light to illuminate something already quite light. Just recently I was reviewing the scene that takes place in the French countryside. What seems to be happening in that passage is that Chad and Marie are already "themselves," although they can become much more "themselves" in the course of their interaction, in their experience with each other in the novel. Even at that late stage in the book Strether is still, by his wild leaps and bounds, becoming illuminated, still becoming aware of new aspects of himself that he's exploring. The light analogy has (you'll pardon the expression) illuminated a whole new part of the landscape—the internal landscape that Strether didn't see before. Every time there is a flash of insight there is a whole new avenue for him to explore. And that's why I think that scene in Gloriani's garden has such immense value.

Notice in the scene that Gloriani is out of sight, and for most of the novel he's *completely* out of sight. He often has very little to do with the "relative" part of the story. He is the pure white light that's underneath. His value lies in what is being reflected outside himself, through all the other characters. Anyway, the goal is set. Strether is given the option of moving toward greater and greater—brighter and brighter—light (or toward interaction of all things as part of the unified field), toward greater self-referral and self-sufficiency, or back to less and less light and darkness. That's what, proceeding from now, happens for the rest of the novel.

CJ: Would you turn now to the question of how all this "motion" of Strether's is related to these balancing factors in the unified field?

JR: We've touched on the idea of the unified field, and I've thought about it, and I've heard some discussion on it since I saw you last. As I said earlier, to unified field theorists the values of everything that exists are different expressions of a unified field: all the values—all the basic components of nature—can be placed in groups and split into two general categories. In 1974, the concept of supersymmetry was introduced—a profound mathematical symmetry principle capable of unifying particles of different spin: the bosons, or force fields, and the fermions, or matter fields. Previously physicists had believed that unification of bosons and fermions was impossible. But it has now been found that an underlying formulation (called the Lagrangian) will allow the two antithetical components to come together into an underlying unity.

CJ: Can you name some of these values or basic components?

JR: Freedom, unboundedness, self-sufficiency, self-referral, invincibility, organizing power, creativity, nourishing capacity, immortality, perfect balance . . . .

CJ: Can you say that when a person transcends "enough" (successively), these qualities that Dr. Hagelin finds in the unified field begin to "show up"? Is this what happened to Strether?

JR: Yes. As one's consciousness grows, one begins integrating all of these different qualities in a perfectly balanced way. To return to the idea of opposing fields that have an underlying unity: I have suggested this before about Woollett and Rome. Let's state it in terms of the unified field: the properties of Woollett *collectively* make it not *one* quality, not a single category, but (call it) a field. And there has to be a "Woollett" field to balance a "Rome" field.

CJ: A "negative" field?

JR: Let's just say a counterbalancing field. Anyway, that's my theory. Of course, there could be other forces at work, a far more complex exchange than this. But in general, Strether's activity is an expression of a balance that occurs in the unification of his own consciousness which is really framed in and supported by a balance in the unified field, or nature as a whole as it includes the unified field. In some respects the physical trip from Woollett to Paris represents a component of "the self traveling within the self," traveling within a field, because the field (the whole unified field) is located everywhere and yet we have to (or Strether has to) be given directionality in order to convey the idea that some motion has taken place. It is motion within the self, within the unified field, in the widest sense from nothingness, or emptiness, to fullness, and in the more particular sense, the motion balances those particular formulations of initial and counterbalancing forces required by the unified field. Since the field has the component of invincibility, once we've located *that* in its fullness—once we have repeatedly transcended until enlightened and therefore are fully "connected" to the unified field—we're just as comfortable in emptiness or even in ignorance, because we're full in ourselves and the field is full in us. Then we see the ignorance in the world to be just a veil, hiding the true fullness [of Being] that's really there despite the appearance of emptiness. After he has reached his highly developed state of consciousness, Strether, knowing this, has no qualms about taking that quality (of fullness) with him out into activity, spreading that quality into the activity of the world no matter what degree of ignorance he encounters at any given time or place.

Motion is an important idea because the momentum that moved him to Paris is an outside force. He was pushed; he was asked to go there and he moved at the request of an individual and by circumstance; we almost get the notion depicted in physics of two billiard balls crashing together. One ball loses all of its momentum by transferring it to the other one. That one goes shooting off. That was the way the original momentum was imparted to the character at the beginning of the novel. But he has exhausted the momentum that carried him to Paris and then he realized the value of just being there in his own consciousness. There is no momentum left in the character to carry him back to where he began except momentum that he generates himself. There's no external stimulus in Paris moving him out, so it must be an internal stimulus, an internal momentum that causes him to move back to Woollett, and that seems to imply the dynamism that results from recognition of the Self combined with the recognition of the unity of all things. You talk about all this in your sixth chapter. It is a state of pure energy that can impart motion or directionality or momentum to individuals and advance them in time and space. Strether moving back to Woollett is the individual moving within himself in an infinitely dynamic way. Again, to go back to an earlier point, you can also call his state "self-referral," because the motion is his Self extending to his Self's farthest reaches! He is not moving anywhere outside [he is "contained in"] his own consciousness. Bear in mind that movement back to Woollett, or movement (should he choose to take it) from Paris to Rome would be a dynamic kind of momentum that's been generated because of a higher state of consciousness.

The next quality of the unified field to come up is self-sufficiency. It's a quality that's interesting to speculate on, because, while Strether was completely dependent on others at the beginning of the book, he has become pretty self-sufficient by the time he encounters Gloriani in Paris, and toward the end of the novel, since he is completely self-sufficient, there's almost no need for him to do anything or be anything in particular in a relative sense. His decision to return to Woollett is really an expression of his own self-sufficiency. He'll be "complete" no matter where he is. He no longer needs Gloriani; he no longer needs that transcendent influence, because he himself is now so thoroughly steeped in it and saturated by it that he can go where he thinks he can do the most good.

*   *   *

In the lecture below, Hagelin clarifies the connection between the two elements, Transcendental Consciousness and the unified field. In this limited space it would be impossible to "prove" such a connection; but his remarks certainly make clear, in largely nontechnical language, how the connection is logical and possible.

Buckminster Fuller often used to make the point that 95% of what we live by in the twentieth century is invisible. Because of the scientific developments that brought this condition upon us, the perspective of man has changed. One result of this change is that we are in a position to recognize phenomena Henry James is treating in his work that we could not even consider before. Hagelin, in a recent lecture at his own university, characterized our present era of change and showed why it prompts a general interest in consciousness by physicists; in doing so he set the stage historically for an equation of the pure consciousness Strether experiences and the contemporary unified field. (After this beginning, his argument goes on for more pages than I am able to offer here. Hence the abrupt ending.)

CONSCIOUSNESS AND THE UNIFIED FIELD[4]

Before discussing the relationship between consciousness and the unified field in detail, I shall attempt to offset at least partially the predisposition against such a comparison resulting from a particular viewpoint characteristic of our age. This predisposition results from more than three centuries of scientific investigation dedicated almost entirely to the analysis of macroscopic, inert matter. The extremely inert and mechanical view of nature that has emerged from the physics of prior centuries defines a certain "paradigm" or world-view which is deeply entrenched in our thinking and in our educational institutions. It seems to preclude the possibility that nature could possess in any fundamental sense the lively and dynamical characteristics that one would normally associate with consciousness.

By the advent of the quantum theory,[5] it was clear that such classical constructs could not apply to the atomic domain. The classical view of the hydrogen atom in which the electron orbits the proton in exact correspondence with celestial mechanics predicts a continuous radiation of electromagnetic energy that would lead to atomic instability. The solution provided by the quantum theory involved a fundamentally new theoretical framework and language of nature more appropriate to the physics of microscopic scales. The vastly greater energy associated with nuclear transitions compared with chemical transformations provides a practical demonstration of the increasing dynamism intrinsic to more fundamental scales. But characteristics other than dynamism can be cited in connection with fundamental scales. Many such properties, including intelligence, arise most naturally in the context of a unified theory. For example, natural law is more concentrated at more fundamental states . . . . Since the laws of nature are the expressions of order and intelligence governing the behavior of natural phenomena, as natural law becomes more concentrated, intelligence becomes more concentrated. If, as particle physicists would have us believe, all the laws of nature have their ultimate origin in the dynamics of the unified field, then the unified field must itself embody the total "intelligence" of nature's functioning.

---

[4] Maharishi International University, 1986

[5] Quantum theory is a mathematical theory of dynamic systems in which dynamic variables are represented by abstract mathematical operators having properties that specify the behavior of the system.

These abstract but nonetheless real properties of "dynamism," and "intelligence" are included to illustrate the fact that many fundamental characteristics of consciousness are increasingly expressed at more fundamental space-time scales. At the same time, much of the *objective* character of macroscopic matter begins to disappear at fundamental scales. The concrete notion of a classical particle is replaced by a more abstract quantum-mechanical wave function, which represents only the probability for a particle to exist. In a second-quantized field theory, even the wave function, which is technically a field, is replaced by a "wave functional or wave functions," which represents the probability that a given field shape exists. Furthermore, in the context of quantum gravity, the essential framework of space-time itself becomes indefinite, being replaced by a quantum-mechanical superposition of space-time metrics. *Thus we see that while certain subjective qualities of existence are becoming more expressed, the concrete and objective nature of existence starts to become more tenuous at fundamental scales* (emphasis, Johnson).

One valid interpretation of this phenomenon is that the distinction between subjectivity and objectivity is less meaningful at microscopic scales. This point has already become clear in the context of quantum measurement, where recent experiments cast severe doubts on any interpretation of the universe based on "local realism." "Realism" implies that objects have their own objective and independent existence apart from the observer; "locality" means that space-time possesses, at least macroscopically, the causal structure defined by Einstein's special relativity. Since most physicists are extremely reluctant to sacrifice relativistic causality, it is generally believed that the assumption of "realism" must be abandoned at the quantum-mechanical level. Quantum-mechanical systems, such as an electron, simply do not have a purely objective existence. The existence of the electron and many of its properties depend intimately upon conventions established by the observer.

Hence the distinction between subject and object, which appears so obvious and unchallengeable at the classical level, is rather ambiguous at the quantum-mechanical level, and may be completely meaningless at the level of super-unification. Since we shall assume that the unified field is the only dynamical degree of freedom present at the super-unified scale, to the extent that a subject-object relationship can be defined there at all, the "observer" and the "observed" must both be found within the dynamical self-interaction of the unified field itself. The unified field is therefore as much a field of subjectivity as a field of objectivity. Hence, the proposed identity between the "objective" unified field of modern theoretical physics, and the "subjective" unified field of consciousness seems better motivated.

Most physicists would be quick to agree that the unified field of modern theoretical physics is the unified source of both subjective and objective existence. This is because most physicists would like to avoid the necessity of introducing anything external to the laws of physics, such as a metaphysical explanation for consciousness, feeling that the unified field should be the dynamical origin of all phenomena. This point of view has been frequently attacked by individuals outside the sciences as being too "reductionistic," i.e., reducing one's subtle experience to the "billiard ball" behavior of elementary particles. This passionate objection probably stems from a misunderstanding of the nature of physics at more fundamental scales, which is not mechanical in the Newtonian sense, but is increasingly subtle and dynamic. Recall that the classical concept of a particle is supplanted at the atomic level by a more abstract and unlocalized wave function in the nonrelativistic quantum theory, which is in turn replaced at subatomic scales by a still more abstract and unlocalized quantum field in a second-quantized theory. Relating subtle mental phenomena to the dynamical behavior of a Lorentz-invariant quantum field might more accurately be described as "expansionism."[6]

*   *   *

EXPLORING THE UNITY OF NATURE: THE "HIGHLIGHTS" IN FULLER FORM

Not long ago, Professor Hagelin gave a report to his University on the progress of physics in uncovering the deepest principles of natural law. He started by saying the unified field approach is based on the principle that the surface diversity of nature emerges from an underlying unity (or, in the terminology of physics, "symmetry"). The deeper the level of nature physics explores, the more unified nature turns out to be. The following is a summation of the rest of his report:

---

[6] For a copy of the complete lecture, write to the Department of Physics, Maharishi International University, Fairfield, Iowa, 52556.

As shown in the figure below, at the nuclear level (see I), four fundamental forces underlie all other forms in nature (see II). Only recently have these forces been shown to be based on one fundamental field (III), a field which comprehends all of creation.

I. 10^{-14} cm

II.   The radioactive force (1)

> Weinberg, Salam, and Glashow developed the unified framework for these two forces.

The electromagnetic (or "weak") force (2)

> Recently it became possible to demonstrate the unification of these two fields by means of a mathematical symmetry called "supersymmetry" and by means of the discovery of a new element particle, the Z-Boson.

The nuclear ("strong") force.

The gravitational force (4)

III.   Supergravity
         Unification of all forces in nature.

This last development followed the recent discovery of a new elementary particle,[7] which, although it appeared for only a fraction of a second (10^{-24} seconds) represented, according to Hagelin, "the reenlivenment of a law of nature that had disappeared from our universe fractions of a second after the big bang and hadn't reappeared since." The discovery of the existence of this particle confirmed the unification of the electromagnetic and weak fields.

But the term "elementary particle" used here, he explained, is a misnomer. The so-called elementary particles are really just exci-

---

[7] The Z-Boson. A Boson is a particle, such as a photon, having zero or integral spin and obeying statistical rules that permit any number of identical particles to occupy the same quantum state (after Jagadis Chandra Bose, Indian physicist). A Fermion (after Enrico Fermi, American physicist) is a particle, such as an electron, proton, or neutron, having half-integral spin and obeying statistical rules requiring that not more than one in a set of identical particles may occupy a particular quantum state.

tations of more abstract and fundamental entities called quantum fields.[8]

Nature appears diverse because only some of these quantum fields are lively on the surface level of life. The "heavy" quantum fields—those which unify the seemingly different laws of nature—function only at very short time and distance scales. "They pervade everything," Hagelin said, "but on a subtle level."

The goal of modern physics is to find one quantum field from which all the others emerge. The final frontier of this program of unification is found at 10^{-35} cm, which is known as the Planck scale. This is the "point value" of physics—the smallest conceivable distance—because at this level the gravitational field becomes so intense that even the familiar structure of space-time dissolves. When physics transcends space and time, it becomes meaningless to speak of smaller distances, or of any sort of distance at all.

The most striking principle arising at the Planck scale is called supersymmetry, which permits the ultimate unification in physics, that of particles of different spin, previously thought to be irreconcilable. According to Hagelin, "this unification based on supersymmetry provides the basis for the emergence of an entirely new and remarkable theoretical model called the unified field, a single field which embodies the grand totality of all the laws of nature as inseparable components of one self-sufficient, infinitely dynamic field."

Thus, modern physics is arriving at an understanding of the ultimate nature of the universe as an unmanifest, unified field [a field of] infinite self-referral, a self-sufficient one; whose "limitless creativity remains a constant reality that can be located at every point in creation." According to Vedic Science, he continued, complete self-referral is the hallmark of consciousness, because only consciousness can know itself. The unified field is thus the field of pure consciousness, the Self.

When physics explores the fine-scale structure of the quantum level of nature, the heavier quantum fields show up and the underlying unity of nature becomes increasingly apparent.

Hagelin continues: "A principle known as spontaneous breaking and restoration of symmetry allows us to look deeply into the

---

[8] Quantum fields have an intrinsic dynamism not found in classical physical fields. The least excited or "vacuum" state of the quantum field (the state of no particles, viewed classically as empty space) is infinitely lively, containing in virtual form all possible excited states of the field simultaneously.

structure of the vacuum and uncover hidden symmetries between laws of nature that had previously been considered absolutely unrelated . . . the intrinsic dynamism characteristic of laws at finer time and distance scales emerges. These heavier laws of nature have been 'frozen out' of the macroscopic world (as the universe has cooled since the big bang). We find that the quantum fields lively in the vacuum are not distinct and separate entities, but are in fact indistinguishable members of one field, one wholeness moving within itself."

Certain methods of meditation make use of this self-referral property to allow one to experience the unified field directly as the least excited state of one's own consciousness.

REFERENCES

Augustine, Saint. *The City of God*. Translated by Marcus Dods. New York: Modern Library, 1950.

Banquet, Jean-Paul. "Spectral Analysis of EEG in Meditation." *Electroencephalography and Clinical Neurophysiology* 35 (1973): 143–51.

Battista, John R. "The Science of Consciousness." In *The Stream of Consciousness: Scientific Investigations into the Flow of Human Experience*, edited by Kenneth S. Pope and Jerome L. Singer, 55–87. New York: Plenum, 1978.

Bhagavad-Gita. Chapters 1–6. A New Translation and Commentary by Maharishi Mahesh Yogi. Baltimore: Penguin Books, Inc., 1967.

Blackwell, Barry, et al. "Transcendental Meditation in Hypertension: Individual Response Patterns." *Lancet*, January 31, 1975, 223–26.

Bloomfield, Harold, Michael Peter Cain, and Dennis T. Jaffe. *TM— Discovering Inner Energy and Overcoming Stress*. Foreword by Hans Selye; Introduction by Buckminster Fuller. New York: Delacourt Press, 1975.

Bucke, Richard Maurice. *Cosmic Consciousness, A Study of the Human Mind*. Secaucus, N.J.: The Citadel Press, 1982.

Campbell, Anthony. *TM and the Nature of Enlightenment*. New York: Harper and Row, 1975.

Clark, R. W. *Einstein, The Life and Times*. New York: World Publishing Co., 1971.

Cohen, J. M. and J. F. Phipps. *The Common Experience*. Boston: Houghton, Mifflin, 1979.

Crews, F. C. *"The Ambassadors." The Tragedy of Manners/Morals Dilemma in the Later Novels of Henry James*. New Haven: Yale University Press, 1957.

Current Research on Sleep and Dreams. U.S. Department of Health, Education and Welfare, Public Health Service, Publication no. 1389. Washington, D.C.: Government Printing Office, 1965.

Dillbeck, Michael C., Garland S. Landrith III, and David W. Orme-Johnson. "The Transcendental Meditation Program and Crime Rate Change in a Sample of Cities." *Crime and Justice* 4 (1981): 25–45.

Edel, Leon. "The Architecture of the New York Edition." *New England Quarterly* 24 (1951): 169–78.

———. *Henry James, The Master, 1909–1916*. New York: J. B. Lippincott Co., 1972.

Farrow, John T., and J. Russell Herbert. "Breath Suspension During the Transcendental Meditation Technique." *Psychosomatic Medicine* 44 (1982): 133–226.

Ferguson, Phil, and John C. Gowan. "TM: Some Preliminary Findings." *Journal of Humanistic Psychology* 16, no. 3 (1976): 51–60.

Fogel, Daniel Mark. *Henry James and the Structure of the Romantic Imagination*. Baton Rouge: Louisiana State University Press, 1981.

Frew, David R. "Transcendental Meditation and Productivity." *Academy of Management Journal* 17 (1974): 362–68.

Fullerton, W. Morton. " 'The Art of Henry James.' A review of *The Novels and Tales of Henry James*. New York ed. 24 vols. London: Macmillan, 1907–1909." *The Quarterly Review* 212, no. 423 (1910): 394–95.

Great Dialogues of Plato. Translated by W. H. D. Rouse. New York: The New American Library, 1956.

Handbook of Imagery, Research and Practice. Edited by Akhter Ahsen and A. T. Dolan. New York: Brandon House, 1985.

Hartman, Ernest. *The Biology of Dreaming*. Springfield, Ill.: Charles C. Thomas, 1967.

Hocks, Richard A. *Henry James and Pragmatistic Thought: A Study in the Relationships Between the Philosophy of William James and Henry James*. Chapel Hill: North Carolina Press, 1974.

Holland, Laurence Bedwell. *The Expense of Vision: Essays on the Craft of Henry James*. Princeton: Princeton University Press, 1964.

Ionesco, Eugene. *Present Past Past Present*. New York: Grove Press, 1971.

James, Henry. *The Ambassadors*. Edited by Leon Edel. Cambridge, Mass.: The Riverside Press, 1960.

——. *The Art of the Novel, Critical Prefaces*. Introduction by Richard P. Blackmur. New York: Charles Scribner's Sons, 1947.

——. "Benvolio." *The Complete Tales of Henry James*. Vol. 3. Edited by Leon Edel. Philadelphia: J. B. Lippincott Co., 1982.

——. *The Future of the Novel: Essays on the Art of Fiction*. Edited by Leon Edel. New York: Vintage Books, 1956.

——. "Is There a Life After Death?" *In After Days*. New York: Harper, 1910.

——. *Letters IV, 1895–1916*. Edited by Leon Edel. Cambridge: Harvard University Press, 1984.

——. *The Notebooks of Henry James*. Edited by F. O. Matthiessen and Kenneth B. Murdock. New York: Oxford University Press, 1961.

——. "Notes on Novelists." *The Portable Henry James*. Rev. ed. Edited by Lyall H. Powers. New York: The Viking Press, 1968.

——. *Portrait of a Lady*. Introduction by R. P. Blackmur. New York: Dell Publishing Co., Inc., 1961.

——. *Portrait of a Lady*. 1881. Afterword by Oscar Cargill. New York: New American Library, 1963.

——. *"Portrait of a Lady."* An Authoritative Text; Henry James and the Novel; Reviews and Criticisms. Edited by Robert D. Bamberg. New York: W. W. Norton and Co., Inc., 1975.

——. "Project of Novel." Abridged. *The Ambassadors:* Appendix. Complete edition: *The Notebooks of Henry James*. Edited by F. O. Matthiessen and Kenneth B. Murdock. New York: Oxford University Press, 1961.

——. *The Spoils of Poynton*. 1888. New York: Dell, 1959.

James, William. *Essays in Radical Empiricism*. Cambridge: Harvard University Press, 1976.

——. *Human Immortality*. See *The Will to Believe*.

——. *The Varieties of Religious Experience: A Study in Human Nature*. New York: Random House, 1929.

————. *The Will to Believe and Other Essays in Popular Philosophy*. 1st ed.; *Human Immortality*. 2d ed. Published in one volume. New York: Dover Publications, Inc., 1956.

Joyce, James. *Ulysses*. New York: Random House, 1941, 1961.

Kant, Immanuel. *The Critique of Practical Reason and Other Writings in Moral Philosophy*. Edited and Introduction by Lewis W. Beck. Chicago: University of Chicago Press, 1949.

Kleitman, Nathaniel. *Sleep and Wakefulness*. Chicago: University of Chicago Press, 1963.

Kuhn, Thomas. *The Structure of Scientific Revolutions*. Chicago: University of Chicago Press, 1970.

La Brie, Ross. "Henry James's Idea of Consciousness." *American Literature* 39 (1968): 517–29.

Long, Robert E. "*The Ambassadors* and the Genteel Tradition: James's Correction of Hawthorne and Howells." *New England Quarterly* 42 (1969): 44–46.

Lubbock, Percy. *The Craft of Fiction*. New York: The Viking Press, 1957.

McLean, Robert. "The Complete Vision: A Study of 'Madame de Mauves' and *The Ambassadors*." *Modern Language Quarterly* 28 (1967): 446–61.

A Manual of Standardized Terminology, Techniques and Scoring System for Sleep Stages of Human Health. Edited by A. Rechtschaffer and A. Kales. Public Health Services Publication 204. Washington, D.C.: Government Printing Office, 1968.

Matthiessen, F. O. *Henry James: The Major Phase*. New York: Oxford University Press, 1963.

Oates, Joyce Carol. "A Terrible Beauty is Born." *New York Times*, August 11, 1985, 29.

Orme-Johnson, David. "Automatic Stability and Transcendental Meditation." *Psychosomatic Medicine* 35 (1973): 341–49.

Orme-Johnson, David, and Christopher T. Haynes. "EEG Phase Coherence, Pure Consciousness, Creativity, and TM-Sidhi Experiences." *International Journal of Neuroscience* 13 (1981): 211–17.

Orme-Johnson, David, Michael C. Dillbeck, R. Keith Wallace, and Garland S. Landrith III. "Intersubject Coherence: Is Consciousness a Field?" *International Journal of Neuroscience* 16 (1982): 203–9.

Orme-Johnson, Rhoda. "Doris Lessing's *The Marriages Between Zones Three, Four, and Five:* An Archetype for the Evolution of Consciousness." Ninth annual Twentieth Century Literature Conference, Louisville, Kentucky, February 1981.

Powers, Lyall. "The Portrait of a Lady: 'The Eternal Mystery of Things.' " *Nineteenth Century Fiction* (1959): 143–55.

Seeman, William, Nidich Sanford, and Thomas Banta. "Influence of Transcendental Meditation on a Measure of Self-Actualization." *Journal of Counseling Psychology* 19 (1972): 184–87.

Stallman, R. W. " 'The Sacred Rage': The Time-Theme in *The Ambassadors." Modern Fiction Studies* 3 (1957): 41–56.

Tanner, Tony. "The Watcher from the Balcony: Henry James's *The Ambassadors." Critical Quarterly* (Spring 1966): 35–52.

Tjoa, Andre. "Meditation, Neuroticism, and Intelligence." *Gedrag: Tijdschrift voor Psychologie [Behavior: Journal of Psychology]* 3 (1975): 167–82.

Van Ghent, Dorothy. *The English Novel: Form and Function.* New York: Holt, Rinehart & Winston, 1953.

Wallace, Robert Keith. "The Physiological Effects of Transcendental Meditation: A Proposed Major State of Consciousness." In *Scientific Research on the Transcendental Meditation and TM Sidhi Program: Collected Papers.* Vol. 1. Edited by David Orme-Johnson, John T. Farrow, and L. H. Domash. Rheinweiler, Germany: MERU Press, 1977.

———. Herbert Benson, and Archie Wilson. "A Wakeful Hypometabolic Physiologic State." *American Journal of Physiology* 221 (1971): 795–99.

Ward, J. A. "*The Ambassadors* as a Conversion Experience." *Southern Review* n.s. 5 (1968): 352–55.

Woolf, Virginia. *The Common Reader.* New York: Harcourt Press, 1925.

Publishers note: The last page of the references was lost between the floppy disk and the typeset machine. We are sorry if the reader is inconvenienced, but we do believe that the tipped in addendum will last as long as the permanent paper.

(RC)

INDEX

ing), 96
and perception, 116, 118–19
personal accounts of, 51–53, 90,
  91, 92 n.4, 114–15
as physiological, 49–50, 118
and the unifed field theory, 153–54
Tree of the Fall, 65
Tree of the Resurrection, 65

Unified Field Theory, 143–47, 152,
  155–60
and consiousness, 145, 155
and light, 148–50
and motion, 151, 153
Unity, of all creation, 33
in diversity, 15, 22–23, 29, 37–38,
  101, 144
of nature, 159
underlying, 141, 157

"Vacuum," 160
Veda, The 110
Vedic Science, 159
Verver, Maggie (char.), 2, 5
Vionnet, Jeanne de, 89
Vionnet, Marie de, 25, 27–30 passim,
  68, 86, 110, 118, 125, 126, 146,
  151
and the affair with Chad, 61–62,
  84, 99, 101–2, 130–35, 137,
  140
her deception of Strether, 98–99
higher consciousness of, 125

as the impetus of Strether's transcendence, 18, 55–58, 61, 89,
  91–95, 100–02, 111–12, 135–37
and Strether's final visit, 97
Strether's opinion of, 83, 84, 88,
  89
Strether's surrender to, 92–94, 109,
  119
as Strether's teacher, 91–93
"Virtuous Attachment," 61, 83–86,
  98–99, 102–3
"Volte Face," 33

Wallace, R. K., 75
Warburton, Lord (char.), 66, 68, 81
Ward, J. A., 3
Weinberg, Steven, 158
W-field, 149 n.2
Winterbourne (char.), 116
Woolfe, Virginia, 46
Woollett, 32, 55, 121, 123, 125, 140
consciousness, 108, 124, 133
experience, 18, 44, 56, 86
philosophy, 17, 19, 29, 35–36, 38,
  40, 42, 113
Strether's return to, 109, 137, 143,
  153
and the unified field theory, 148,
  152, 154
Wordsworth, William, 51, 53

Z-Boson, 158 n.7
Z field, 149 n.2